Born on Tuesday, August 1st, 1967, at midnight at Middlesex Hospital, Malcolm David Bateup, previously Trower, Leo the Lion birth sign, has had considerable challenges in his life which have made him into the man, father and husband he is today. During school, he experienced serious bullying, family break-up, divorce and, later, various career setbacks, loss and bereavements, which has tested his resilience and resolve. A former engineer, he completely changed direction of his career during the recession in the 1980s; he undertook voluntary work with people with learning difficulties and mental health problems, as well as studying with the Open University with the plan to work with people rather than making things. Between 1994 and 2000, he successfully completed two degrees in Psychology and Social Policy, respectively, as well as two further diplomas in Health and Social Welfare, and Applied Social Science and later attended a Business School, undertaking further studies in Professional Judgement and Decision Making, and Managing Roles and Relationships. This study changed everything and since 1996, he has worked in the Health Field as a Social Worker Advocate, Recovery Worker and, currently, as a Psychotherapist after completing further advanced professional qualifications in Psychotherapy in 2010. Malcolm started MB Counselling Services in 2011 and feels that setting up his own business was the best decision he ever made, apart from marrying his wife only last year. As a relationship expert, Malcolm works at consulting rooms all over Sussex and focuses his expertise and professionalism using an integrative approach which uses many different powerful therapeutic techniques that can be adapted to change, depending on perceived relationship problems.

Malcolm believes there is a book in everyone and had always wanted to write a book himself that helps people to learn from their mistakes and lead fulfilling lives. Malcolm's philosophy, spirituality and faith, has always been to want to give and help people. So, it was not a surprise when he met Nicola Anne, who became his wife in 2017; a nurse herself for over 25 years, who has given so much to others and shares his values in life. As you will read, like-minded people attract each other and meet people with same beliefs and values.

Dedication

I dedicate this book to all the people who want to 'Live their lives like they have lived it before'. Also, to my beautiful wife, who has been so supportive and inspirational and who motivated me to finish it during a difficult period in my life. Also, special thanks to my family and friends who I love very much and hope they find more happiness and success and live their lives. To my special son, who loves writing and singing, and inspired me to write this book. I also wanted to share with the world my knowledge, not just being a professional therapist, but also to write a book that was simple and easy to read and understand. I am also sharing significant life events linked to all the chapters which I hope you enjoy. Part of living your life is to have lived through difficult experiences and learn from those memories. I was severely bullied at school, which affected my confidence. This experience and trauma also made me determined and develop resilience and inner strength to be the person I am today, as well as becoming a therapist myself. Today, my trademark is to wear silver shoes to remind me of that trauma and to celebrate difference, diversity, uniqueness and creativity and another reason to stand up to bullying and motivate me to complete this book. If this is happening to you, this book will remind you that you are a unique individual, able to realise your potential and celebrate your uniqueness and remind you that you are amazing and capable of doing wonderful things in your life. I challenge you to wear something silver (shoes if you dare!) for a week and stand up to bullying and celebrate diversity. This book also needed to be completed because it was written during an extremely difficult period when, sadly, we lost a friend to suicide and my wife's father also lost his battle and is now looking down from heaven, back in the arms of his wife, Pat, watching from above and proud of their family. So, to all these experiences and people that have motivated me to complete this book in their memories. In all their legacy, I dedicate this book to those special people we have sadly lost. The aim of this book is like giving a stranger who has been hurt by life the holy grail of knowledge to enable them to change their thinking and improve the quality of their life. I really hope this book makes a difference to your life. In short, if you apply even some of the tips in this book, then you will likely lead a more fulfilling, healthier and successful life in the future.

The last chapter brings everything together and shows how everything in this book is connected to enable you to live your life like you have lived it before.

"Life just is, let go, let it happen and just be and live life for the moment." – Johnson, 1890

Malcolm Bateup

Live Your Life like You Have Lived It Before

AUSTIN MACAULEY PUBLISHERS™

LONDON • CAMBRIDGE • NEW YORK • SHARJAH

A CIP catalogue record for this title is available from the British Library.

ISBN 9781528907927 (Paperback)
ISBN 9781528907934 (Hardback)
ISBN 9781528907941 (E-Book)

www.austinmacauley.com

First Published (2018)
Austin Macauley Publishers Ltd
25 Canada Square
Canary Wharf
London
E14 5LQ

Acknowledgements

To all the people who challenge bullying, stigma and celebrate diversity.

A special 'thank you' to the Open University that enabled me to change my career and become a psychotherapist helping people today.

To all the mental health charities, most notably Mind and Sussex Oakleaf, who do amazing work.

To all the therapists in the world who do wonderful work.

To NHS, who carry out incredible work daily to make us all better.

The pride I have for my wife, an amazing nurse who has carried out over 25 years of dedication to the service and helped so many people during that time.

To my son who is amazing, and I love him. And to Autism.

Special acknowledgment to all my family who have supported me and believed in me.

To all couples and single people, I hope you find happiness, love and fulfilment, and you all live your life like you have lived it before.

If you have been bullied or put down, don't listen to them, as you are a unique individual capable of doing something amazing with your life.

Table of Contents

Introduction

We come to this world as babies with no manual on how to live our lives. A bit like a computer with no instructions. By exploring our world as we grow up, we learn by mistakes; some of which are vital and have consequences that affect the rest of our lives. Wouldn't it be great if we could live our life like we have lived it before? This book is a practical guide on how to become successful and not make those errors and fall into the trap everyone does which ultimately results in failure and unhappiness. Worse still, poor health and wellbeing are more likely as a result due to stress and a shorter life expectancy.

As we all know, stress kills and there is nothing more stressful than problems in our life and the stress and unhappiness they cause. You only must look at a busy roundabout to see that everyone is rushing with no time to stop and think. Everyone needs to, it seems, get to a destination immediately, but are stuck in the rut of congestion and road rage and think they must do the same as everyone else because this is what everyone else does. Significantly with no consideration for other road users or their journeys. However, in short, you don't have to be angry people with your adrenalin through the roof and follow the pied piper and the rest of the crowd and do what everyone else does to be successful. Taking a chance and doing something different usually makes you stand out from the crowd or that busy traffic at the roundabout and gain that job or relationship that you craved and deserved. Most importantly, investing in yourself is not selfish. 'It's the most worthwhile thing you can do'. As unique individuals, we owe ourselves the opportunity to do something different and special and amazing, and most importantly to be happy and contented with our unique and beautiful gift of life.

Chapter 1
Change Your Thinking and Transform Your Life

I believe that if we changed our distorted thinking, we could completely transform our lives. In cognitive behavioural therapy (CBT), we challenge distorted thinking which is also described as self-destructive behaviour. However, you don't have to be in therapy to transform your life. We can challenge our thinking, change our thinking and change our lives by following just a few simple steps. In short, to stop thinking negatively and replace with positive thinking. With new positive beliefs and positive expectations, we believe and expect good things to happen to us. There is plenty of evidence through studies that people who have done this have become successful almost overnight. Just think how simple this is! Negative thinking attracts negative thoughts and unhappiness in our lives. In contrast, if we challenge that negative thinking that psychologists call distorted thinking or self-sabotaging behaviour and replacing our thoughts with positive thoughts we can have more constructive positive lives.

In the story of Noah, like other stories in the first 11 chapters of Geneses in the Bible, it tells us that human beings have an inherent tendency towards violence both towards their fellow human beings and towards the creation itself. So, do you choose life or to self-destruct before you have even started? Unfortunately, many of us do not necessarily choose to self-destruct but circumstances out of our control happen and cause us to push the self-destruct button. However, some things are in our control and we do have a choice of how to behave and react. This is where our values, personality and unique characteristics make us who we are today, some from life experience out of our control and some from what we can control.

It is vital we are answerable to the actions, so we can take control and hold ourselves accountable for our self-destructing behaviour. In relationships, a couple always believes that actions speak louder than words. In short, it's about what you do, not what you say.

We come into the world like a beautiful computer with no instruction manual, so it is so easy to go off in the wrong direction. However, by changing our thought process we can stay happy, healthy and meet like-minded people who share our beliefs, values and attitudes. Studies have shown people that challenge there distorted thinking become happier, live more fulfilling lives and can also earn more money, live longer and avoid illness far longer than negative thinking people.

Once we get into what therapist's call negative automatic thoughts and or self-destructive behaviour patterns of thinking, they are rigid and hard to change during therapy. Therefore, let's find a way to not have them in the first place and change direction and a negative life journey by thinking clearer, wiser and creatively and change this negative cycle before it is too late and distorted to change to a more fulfilling, positive, healthy way of life.

Changing your thinking and more importantly having the knowledge to know how to do this is possible, and is very powerful. We don't have to follow the crowd and be unhappy and fail in life. We don't have to do the same as others do. It is too easy to just act like a herd of sheep running off the cliff to self-destruction. We don't have to live a life that everyone else does, we can simply choose life and to live as unique human beings with the ability to be successful, loving, beautiful people and to share our teachings, wisdom and knowledge with others. Let's look at our uniqueness; studies have shown that the chances of having the same finger prints as the next person are a billion to one. A study by Galton in 1892, who first pioneered finger prints, showed one in 64 million probability of two people having identical finger prints, demonstrating human uniqueness. Later, when DNA was developed by Professor Jeffrey in 1986, it showed this figure of uniqueness was one billion to 1 in a world population of 7 billion. Therefore, as well as accurate to catch criminals, it also demonstrates uniqueness. Therefore, we don't have to follow everyone and we all are a unique special precious human being capable of doing something unique and extraordinary with our lives.

The chances of someone having the same finger prints as you are over a billion to one, therefore, that is how different we all are so why do we do the same and just follow like sheep making the same mistakes and errors leading to unhappiness and failure.

Our thinking affects our relationships, careers, money, who we meet, and attract in our lives and the experiences, memories and beliefs are all part of our thinking and dominant thoughts. Indeed, all our relationships and life choices are made up of how we think and feel. So, we don't have to be the same and follow and can think differently and have better outcomes in life. In short, more success and happiness.

Chapter 2
It's Okay to Make Mistakes

Learning by mistakes makes us closer to understanding how to do it right and be a success. Critics laughed at Edison's light bulb theory. They said, "Why do you keep going after so many failings."

Edison replied, "You don't know how the world works, young man. I am 1093 times closer to finding out how to make it work and be successful."

Many thought we would still be in candle light, but Edison knew different, and as they say on his 1094th time, he got it right and invented the light bulb, literally lit up the world. "I have not failed. I've just found 1093 ways that won't work."

Many of life's failures are people who did not realise how close they were to success when they gave up.

I am the kind of person who does not like to carry baggage. In fact, I just like to move forward, you can't change the past but can change your future. It's well-known that people fear failure, and this includes mistakes and getting it wrong and the feelings attached which makes us feel bad and affects our self-confidence and mental health. However, once we realise it is the most perfectly natural thing in the world in making mistakes to progress and develop our confidence, and our belief in our ability will enable us to be successful and not feel a failure in the future. Next time we get something wrong, we will say it is okay. It is okay as it makes us closer to getting it right. It's all about learning and problem solving to find a solution. If you accept you got it wrong, then you are halfway there to success. Once you are aware that it is okay to get it wrong, you do not feel as bad.

Another important part of not feeling a failure and that it is okay to make mistakes is what psychologists describe as self-worth. In short everyone wants to feel they are liked and indeed loved. Significantly, if you don't love yourself or at least like yourself how you can get other people to love and like you? It is important to stay positive because beauty comes from the inside out. As Fred said in *First Dates*, "There is only one happiness in this life, to love and be loved."

However, some mistakes just have greater consequences than others. But you don't have to let the result of one mistake be the thing that defines you. It was one thing to make a mistake; it was another thing to keep making it. What do you first do when you learn to swim? You make mistakes, do you not? And what happens? You make other mistakes, and when you have made all the mistakes you possibly can without drowning—and some of them many times over—what do you find? That you can swim! Well, life is just the same as learning to swim! Do not be afraid of making mistakes, for there is no other way of learning how to live! I thought it was a good idea when I was 17 to have a perm like my idol Kevin Keegan in the later '70s just before I won an under 17 snooker championship and was being photographed by the local paper which was a shock to my family and very funny at the time. Thankfully, like everyone it's okay to make mistakes. The important thing is to learn from mistakes and in my case, this was the last perm I ever had, although, there was a brief dabble with brill cream from another idol Ray Reardon—another bad hair day.

If you are still not convinced, it's okay to make mistakes; these famous people also think it is perfectly okay.

"Anyone who has never made a mistake has never tried anything new."
Albert Einstein

"Freedom is not worth having if it does not include the freedom to make mistakes."
Mahatma Gandhi

"Never interrupt your enemy when he is making a mistake."
Napoléon Bonaparte

"Mistakes, obviously, show us what needs improving. Without mistakes, how would we know what we had to work on?"
Peter Mcwilliam

"Experience is the name everyone gives to their mistakes. Nowadays most people die of a sort of creeping common sense, and discover when it is too late that the only things one never regrets are one's mistakes."
Oscar Wilde

"All men make mistakes, but a good man yields when he knows his course is wrong, and repairs the evil. The only crime is pride."
Sophocles

Chapter 3
Everyone Is Searching for Something

This is true everyone is searching for something. Usually the meaning of life through religion faith or following something such as a football team. The reason they are all searching is to find the ultimate to be happy and content. What are you searching for? Most people want happiness, success and money.

I supported the same football team for 40 years. Liverpool Football Club as a child made me happy and to be fair they had a great deal of success. Sadly, this success did not continue into the millennium and my search for happiness through sport has been lost. What I realised at this point of my life is you cannot rely on others for happiness. Let's be honest, I was not born when England won the 1966 World Cup and probably haven't got long to witness them succeeding again. However, since writing this book, Gareth Southgate with his famous waistcoat and the new-look youthful England Team gave us all an amazing ride in the glorious hot-summer of 2018. Again, near yet so far. So, as I said I learnt to realise that it's you that makes you happy. Of course, people can come into your life and make you happy, but it starts with *you.* Once you are happy and contented with yourself, have peace of mind and happy with who you are you can begin on your happiness journey. Happiness comes from within and once you have found happiness that you were searching for you will attract good things and people in your life.

The most important thing I learnt early on was important thing is to not follow the crowd and believe in your own ability and know what you are searching for. Once you know what you are searching for, formulate a plan to achieve it. Whilst it is okay to go with the flow more people are successful if they have put a plan together and set goals and strategies of how to make work and become successful. Shankly once famously said, "Football is a simple game." The late Brian Clough historically quoted, "It only takes a second to score a goal." For me, these are perfect examples in keeping it simple. You can make life as simple or complicated as you choose. This book enables you to avoid complications and live your life like you have lived it before.

I think everyone goes through chapters in their life and there was a time when I wasn't feeling terribly positive about what I was contributing, or wasn't feeling as if I was going in the direction I wanted, and I re-evaluated what I was doing.

Everyone searches for happiness. They look to material items to fill the emptiness in the centre of their chest. Capitalist values of consumerism promote the acquisition of material goods at the expense of emotional wellbeing. Listen to the dominant cultural narrative, "Just buy a new car house or a new pair of shoes, it'll make you happy." When you seek happiness through material objects, you'll never find it.

Here's three other ways people search for happiness:

1. Relationships

If you're dependent on someone else to feel okay about yourself, then you're looking for happiness in the wrong places. Relationships are beautiful when two whole people meet and share their lives, but are problematic when people are using others to avoid their issues. You can mask your unhappiness, but not for long.

2. Exciting Experiences

While, traveling and adventures are one of life's greatest treasures, they should enrich your life rather than be the source of all contentment. When you're dependent on external events for happiness, it's difficult to create a positive state without exciting experiences. True happiness can be found in 'average' daily life.

3. Admiration, Recognition and Approval

Many people search for happiness by chasing success. Whether financial security or promotions, we think that if people like us, we'll feel satisfied. Just take Facebook and Instagram, people crave to feel that they are loved and liked. In short, you need attention, and admiration to make you feel better in the short term. Unfortunately, when you don't receive that constant stream of attention, you're forced to sit with your underlying unhappiness. Fame and approval doesn't bring lasting happiness. We seek happiness because we're brainwashed. Our cultural conditioning tells us that happiness is something external.

We've been told that we, ourselves, are not enough. Whether it's through relationships, exciting experiences, admiration, or material objects, we think that if we acquire something outside of ourselves we'll finally feel complete.

When we seek happiness, we assume that it is something we lack.

This creates a lack of consciousness that deepens your suffering. Your energetic state tells the universe, "I'm incomplete, inadequate, and want more and I lack experiences." If you identify with this state of less-than, you reinforce and create the very emptiness you seek to fulfil. This identity creates the dilemma of unhappiness.

Here are six steps to discover happiness:

1. Realise That You Are Complete

You are enough! Sure, you have flaws, we all do, but waking up each day is a miracle. Instead of taking precious moments for granted, view them as unique opportunities to engage in self-growth. Practice feeling wholeness and love radiating from the centre of your being, and appreciate the trivial things that make each day worth living.

2. Recognise That Happiness Is Always Present

When you relax and stop stressing over unimportant details, you find happiness. The more you strain to force pleasure into your life, the less happy you feel. Rather than artificially manufacturing a situation to make happiness, try to allow it to enter your life.

3. Live in the Moment

When you stay grounded in the present, you remain open to bliss. Instead of focusing on the past or obsessing about the future, be centred in the here-and-now. Happiness is something that spontaneously emerges when you view the world through the eyes of love, so commit to loving the moment you're in, rather than the moments to come.

4. Prioritise Physical Health

Your body contributes to wellbeing. When you fill your body with toxins, it creates health problems that lead to increase in suffering. If you neglect your body by not exercising, you manufacture an unhealthy environment and invite problems into your life. Focus on eating healthy foods, exercising, staying hydrated, and getting appropriate sleep to help your body continue to support your happiness.

5. Flex Your Mental Health

Thoughts impact your emotions, behaviour, and the way you experience reality. Think of your mental wellbeing like a muscle: the more you exercise, the stronger it'll become. Grow your mental health by engaging in therapy and meditating.
As you learn to release pent up energy and experience inner peace, you'll feel lighter and happier throughout the day.

6. Discover True Happiness

Don't allow yourself to be fooled by your culture. Capitalism wants you to feel incomplete, so you continue purchasing materials and make the one-percent wealthier. Rather than identifying with this emptiness, realise that you are enough. Happiness is always available when your mind, body, and spirit are aligned in the here-and-now. Surrender to the present moment, and feel the happiness that's been there the whole time. My meaning of life is that we are here to teach the next generation and pass on knowledge to the next generation to make them better in the future.

Armed with the knowledge that we are unique and can change and do amazing different things from the previous chapter and with the tools of this chapter suddenly our searching does not become just random and has structure, meaning and purpose and in short, a plan which is likely to end in success and happiness, fulfilment, contentment, peace of mind and fabulous personal and spiritual growth. For me, everyone is searching for the meaning of life.

"The meaning of life is to teach the next generation by passing on knowledge and wisdom to make them better."
Bateup M 2016

Chapter 4
People Desire What They Can't Have

Should there be a different title for people who desire what they can't have? In a world of so much demand, expectations wanting, needing and desiring more than ever before, should you be able to have everything in life? Is it possible to have everything you desire in our busy life? Life just isn't like that, as there will always be difficulties and disappointment, making errors, which is all part of learning and development to become successful and happy. This is an important lesson to learn from an early age. If you think you can always get what you want, then you are setting yourself up to fail and result in unhappiness. I am giving you a reality check, the tools to understand and learn if you haven't already the hard way by upsetting people and yourself that you cannot always fulfil your desires. Just like the Rolling Stones' song, 'you can't always get what you wanted' it is very true. This may sound negative but it's very positive to learn that you can't have everything. Too often, the thing you most want most is the one thing you can't have.

Desire can leave you heart broken, it wears you out. Desire can wreck your life, literally. But as tough as wanting something can be, the people that suffer the most are those who know what they want. Just as people want jobs they cannot have, salaries they cannot earn, cars they cannot afford, people may desire attractive alternatives more and desire their current relationship partner less when they are placed in situations that limit their ability to tend to attractive alternatives. There have been social psychology experiments that have measured attractiveness in a potential mate. In an experiment involving looking at attractive faces participants reported less satisfaction and more positive attitudes towards fidelity than people who could peep at all the faces equally. People also seem to be attracted to facial features from parents from being born attracted to the mother and father as it feels safe and warm, as explained in John Bowlby's attraction theory for secure attachments.

Going back to the Rolling Stones song, 'You can't always get what you want you may get what you need'. This is the ideas of wants and needs. However, what you really wanted is out of your reach. For example, like a person you fancied but it's too late once you realise you liked them because now they are living with someone else. In short, you never know what you have got until it's gone. What is it that you really want? The affections of another person or a dream job. It could just be something you can't afford or is out of your reach like a lovely pair of shoes. You know the example in the film *Pretty Woman*, 'You can't afford it', a judgement without knowing anything about her apart from the clothes she was wearing. When you don't get what you want or desire, what you want can cause severe damage to you psychologically and affect self-esteem in thinking you are not liked, loved or worthy. When you don't get what you want, it causes what psychologists call 'heightened attention'. When something is hard, even forbidden, you immediately pay more attention to it. Notice when you are restricted next time, or something is out of your reach, how you react. Do you focus on it? Yes, of course you do. Studies have shown that in relationships, this makes you more desirable to the opposite sex. If you can't have that person, you want them more. You desire it more, until it's burning and all your focus and attention is on achieving that desire. You become obsessive. Secondly, you become what psychologists call perceived scarcity. When something is scarce and in short supply, its perceived value increases. You want it more because you think other people also want it. If you have ever bided on eBay, for example, you know this experience well; the last-minute bids on the auction as you get excited as they spiral upwards only to be dashed at the end by a late bid. The more you are willing to bid the more you will pay. It becomes: "I must have it and why should that person have it instead of me." Your inner brat comes out at any price.

The next stage of desire is 'psychological reactance'. People don't like to be told they can't have it or can't do something. It is related to not wanting to be controlled by others and that the situation must be unfair if I don't get what I want. It becomes heightened emotion and behavioural as both emotions and unhelpful behaviour is played out. Therefore, being armed with all the above knowledge it is vital that you can develop strategies that don't make you feel like a failure if you don't get what you want. This comes with self-acceptance that you can't always get what you want but think like the song, focus on need and get what you need not desire, as desires are destructive and can break relationships, making you upset or hurt and is destructive to everyone. The behavioural component is what you do about it, which is usually a rebellious reaction as you feel threatened at not being able to achieve your desires, which makes you feel unhappy. You see this with teenagers whose parents have forbidden them to date certain people or stay out late. Again, the controlling behaviour from parents is to keep them safe but controlled. This is the same behaviour to when you see a wet paint sign, you get the desire to touch it to see what would happen, but most of all, it's not that you would be covered in wet paint, it's the 'I will not be controlled and told what I can and cannot do'. Next time when you don't get what you want, ask yourself whether the above factors influence your desire. If so, let go of the pursuit and stay happy, contented and blessed with what you do have. Your inner brat may not be happy but to quote the song from the Rolling Stones, 'you may find just what you need'.

I often thought about desire and want to do a whole book on it as it is a vital part of our happiness and unhappiness if we can channel the desire positively and let go. There are so many examples on why people desire what they can't have. For example, that new pair of high heel shoes in the window with a high price tag. The *sensible you* think's that is too expensive and walks away. The *reflective you* thinks, 'I will try and find a way to afford them and save up'. The *risk-taking you* thinks, 'I really want them but even though I can't afford them I am going to have them'. Especially, if the shop keeper said they are very expensive and remember that scene in *Pretty Woman*, "They are expensive you won't be able to afford them." Which *you* are you?

That *you* is also linked to personality traits of extroversion and introversion. In short, extroverts will always take a risk and gamble and not care about the circumstances and more likely to buy those shoes in the shop window and face consequences such as getting into debt.

Receiving a rejection either before or after a dating experience makes that person more desirable, as you can't have them and you want them and desire that person and will try hard to get them to like you and love you. This is another reason why people desire what they can't have. So, my advice to you is to keep people on their toes and not be easy to date and this will make you far more desirable. Dating is a game where men enjoy the challenge of a chase.

If you like them, make them wait. Respect yourself and this will boost your self-esteem but at the same time, make you more desirable to the opposite sex. The green-eyed monsters called jealousy and envy, where two people, who are involved in a long-term broken, sexless and loveless relationships, find they are attracted to each other and have the desire for an affair to meet those needs. They find out that what they want is gone and they can't have that anymore, and that grass is not greener on the other side. "Pleasure is temporary and fleeting; stop chasing fireworks and start building constellations."

However, work hard for what you want because it won't come to you without a fight. You must be strong and courageous and know that you can do anything you put your mind to.

If somebody puts you down or criticises you, just keep on believing in yourself and turn it into something positive.

Chapter 5
No Action Is Action in Its Self

"No act is sufficient, nor is its meaning so obvious that it would require no expression at all."

It is very important to learn that no action can be a good thing. In short, no action is an action. For example, we often make mistakes, largely due to pressure, it happens to me as well, when we act without thinking properly it leads to consequences. We often think that an action can bring the mind to awareness. We put action against action. We think that there are good actions and bad actions, meaningful actions and meaningless actions.

Let me say something, "No action can ever obliterate another action." Actions do nothing to the quality of the mind. It is our quality of our minds where the action is done.

You can take a shower, a bath. Now, the bath doesn't cleanse you. The real question is, what is the mind that is entering this action? Where is this action coming from? You say, 'meaningful travelling', where is the meaning coming from? What kind of mind? Because after all, you will supply the meaning, right? And you will determine whether it is meaningful or meaningless.

You are the judge, you are the advocate and you are standing in the dock. You must realise that once you have labelled something as meaningful, who is anybody else to call it meaningless? And you are convinced that this action, be it travelling or anything, is meaningful. Now it's meaningful, so meaningful . . . I am living in that.

Moral science has always taught this to us: to look at our actions. No, looking at our actions is one thing, but trying to modify actions is a different thing. You can *observe* the action. And observing the action helps you realise something. But you cannot look at action with the intent of transforming it.

"Nothing is the origin of heaven and Earth," Lao Tzu. "Emptiness which is conceptually liable to be mistaken for sheer nothingness is in fact the reservoir of infinite possibilities," D T Suzuki.

"We came spinning out of nothingness, scattered stars like dust," Rumi.

They were all able to tune into the field of potential through meditation, the art of doing 'nothing'. However, doing nothing is not bad it can be a good thing. There is something in nothing, which is everything. It is the source of creation itself from nothing. Doing mindful activities is doing nothing and fulfils us with deep joy. The key is awareness of what action you are doing in this case nothing is action. Socrates once said, "The only true wisdom is knowing that you know nothing about nothing." Therefore, putting mindful meditation into practice suddenly, the theory of nothing is life and creation itself and being aware that nothing and doing nothing is important is the key to lasting happiness. Doing nothing enables us to think clearer and make better decisions rather than just reacting which usually always results in irrational actions which have adverse consequences.

If we just reflected and had time to digest the issue and thought about it, we would have clarity of thinking and more likely to do or say the right thing which would be beneficial to everyone.

In a relationship, we often react without thinking which always ends up in upsetting people we love. This is important too, once we open our mouths and say something you cannot take it back.

Therefore, words matter, "Your words are more important than your thoughts."

What we say will influence others which maybe irretrievable and end up in upset argument, and in some cases, relationship breakdown. So, my simple advice to you is to stop, take a breath and think before reacting. Don't be afraid to do nothing and give yourself more time to make the right decision.

Don't get pressured into making snap decisions that can cause unhappiness and need further time and work to undo. You may think all the above is waffle but it is in mathematics, philosophy and morals passed down from the ages. In short, if you learn or take anything from this chapter, remember, no action stops conflict, wars and breakdown in relationships. Reaction matters, "It's not what happened it's how you react that matters."

People who have developed the ability to not react and think before they act have always had better outcomes to their lives. In short, "Once it's out, it's out." You can't take it back if you have said something hurtful which can cause or influence the happiness of another. Most vitally, it will also have a consequence on your happiness.

For example, such as what you said could result in the breakdown or even loss of a relationship. If only you thought before being a hot head and said something you now regret, with nowhere to go with that action other than apologising and/or facing the consequences of that instant thinking and reaction. Therefore, use non-action in a positive way instead. For a start, you haven't upset your partner yet as you haven't come out in rage and said something in the heat of the moment you will regret which will probably cost you the relationship. I too have made this mistake and thinking I can just apologise. Even being totally sincere, this is not enough and it diminishes that spark, love and that relationship. All the memories and experiences you shared go up in a puff of smoke. So, give yourself time to think.

We all have been in at least more than one relationship in our lives and as a result, sadly will have come across jealousy and envy. Previous partners and relationships know a lot about us and as a result know how to push our buttons. No action works just as well with these kinds of people who wish to cause harm to a new relationship. When there are children involved sadly, as a therapist I have come across this problem too often, children are used to hurt others but it is the children that suffer. Again, by simply not responding or engaging and carrying out no action will not get the reaction from a previous partner and prevent a scene and most importantly hurt to vulnerable children from a family break up. Also, this jealous behaviour is a sign that your relationship is healthy, and you are happy and contented, and the other person sadly has not moved on and is resentful and is trying to still have a hold over you especially from a previous controlling relationship. No action prevented wars in the past and it works the same way with controlling relationships with previous partners out to cause havoc. Simply say no and carry out the no action is action and they will go away and kill them with kindness as they will not know how to deal with your new learnt behaviour from this book and you have less stress and healthier relationships in the future.

This is my 5-way reflection and action plan that has helped others.

1. No action is an action. Do nothing, give yourself time to breathe and reflect overnight and give yourself more chance to say the right diplomatic response which you can both work through.

2. Once you have reflected, think and feel what you want to say and practice saying it. 'The empty chair' technique used by Eric Berne is a useful therapy technique where the individual can say what he or she likes to the empty chair knowing they are safe and secure and won't receive a horrible response back. This works well in domestic violence, anger management and relationship breakdown to understand what the other person is feeling and most importantly, how it made them feel and the consequences of their actions.

3. Talk it through. This is as simple as that but respect each other's feelings.

4. Agree a plan to work through and improve the disagreements in the relationship.

5. Make up. In short make love, not war. As already mentioned non-action has prevented wars. With today's leaders with the power to just push the button, this response is even more prominent and vital to keep a cool head which is the same in relationship as loved ones know how to push your buttons.

Chapter 6
Stand out from the Crowd and Be Different

So why do people stand out from the crowd and why is it important to be different? Let's say if you saw a photo with one person turning around. This is simple that person chose to move in a different direction. You need not always walk on the road travelled by everybody else. Try walking on the road not taken and you will realise how people recognise you for your uniqueness and individuality. Don't lose yourself. You can't make everyone happy. And if you try, you will lose yourself. Don't run after happiness. "Your obsession from finding happiness stops you from getting it."

Individuality is achieved by being unique. You need not always follow people. You are free to put your own ideas, your opinions and your talents. People are not interested in observing the same things. They are interested in something different. So, how to be that person.

Be Confident:

Imagine a group of people being beaten up by a person in turns. A person among them confidently goes up to him and protests. Who stood out in a crowd?

Do Something New:

In a dance competition, all participants did their classical number. And then comes a girl in her hip hop style. Who stood out in a crowd? Obviously, her performance will be remembered more.

Start Exploring:

Be it your hobbies or anything try doing new things in your area of interest. The experience you get is immense.

Be a Trendsetter, Not a Trend Follower.

I found how vital it is to stand out from the crowd at a recent job interview. After failing many times, not as much as Edison, it was frustrating and demoralising. I thought I need to do something different. Something that makes me stand out from the crowd especially as I had failed over 10 job interviews and put in so much work, time, effort and preparation; all for nothing. Although the presentation asked to develop a plan of how to run a group session, I turned it completely on its head and focussed on an empowerment group which showed how all the other groups would fit in to help promote the whole service. In short, I thought of a whole and holistic approach.

What can I do for this company? Of course, I got the job and when I received feedback, the manager told me my presentation stood out from all the others as it was different and took a risk and cleverly turned the question on its head. They said they were impressed with my different, out-of-the-box thinking, and this creativity would benefit their company.

Creativity in short is just connecting things. Different things other people have not thought of before.

When you ask creative people how they did something, they feel a little guilty because they didn't really *do* it, they just *saw* something, something a bit different from everyone else's tunnel vision. It seemed obvious to them after a while. That's because they could connect experiences they've had and synthesise new things.

And the reason they could do that was that they've had more experiences, or they have thought more about their experiences than other people.

I have found out that now I am comfortable with my identity and love my uniqueness and creativity to do tasks differently, that opportunities have come my way. As well as the career successes, I also found success in love by using the same techniques of doing things differently. In short, not being boring and focusing what makes me a unique individual made me stand out from the rest of the possible suitors that potential mate was looking for. For a start, after a difficult divorce I didn't follow the crowd and live in another house. I couldn't afford to buy a house or even rent a flat but instead, I thought creatively and out of my usual comfort zone and decided even though I know nothing about boats, I would live on one and write this book as it happens. That is what I did, it gave me an adventure but also enabled me to think more creatively about me and about life. I found I did not need material possessions, I focused on being a good person, a giving person to others having quality friendships and relationships and strong family, moral and religious values. Having all this and feeling that I was blessed rather than resentful enabled me to meet the love of my life and now my wife. My dating profile was totally unique but as it was unique it attracted many potential future partners. The most important thing I learnt by dating is how much people for a better word lie or exaggerate about age and status, but I stayed true to myself. If you must do this, it is your self-esteem and confidence and perhaps identity that need working on. For me, honesty is always the key to finding long lasting love and commitment. Without the foundation of trust in which honesty plays its part, you will be set up to fail and dishonesty can only destroy a relationship.

As the great actor Woody Allen once said, "Be careful what you say and if you get drunk the previous night make sure you always tell the truth." That tickled me pink but as well as the obvious humour, there is a clear message. So just stay true to yourself. Remember! A unique individual with individual qualities and focus on your uniqueness and you will find love.

Chapter 7
Resilience Is the Key

Life is difficult and sometimes things go wrong. It maybe problems with a relationship, loss of job and with it our status and purpose in life or the sad death of a love one that knocks us for six from a terrible loss, just a few examples. However, as humans we were born with built-in survival skills, when we are under threat we engage in what is known as 'defence mechanisms'. The two I am going to focus on are 'fight or flight' and 'resilience'.

Churchill once famously quoted, "If you are going through hell drive straight through it." In our darkest days before the impossible task of evacuating Dunkirk, Churchill also significantly said, "Success is not final, Failure is not final. It is the courage to continue that counts." Winston Churchill, 1940.

In the original Rocky film, his coach said, "It's not being hit that counts it is that you keep getting up." For me, resilience is just this that you learn by adverse difficult experiences; the more you experience the more resilient you will become and the more you will get yourself off the canvas and keep going. Our fight or flight defence mechanism and our ability to fight or flight enables us to survive and to show resolve. We develop through our mental tool box the awareness to have a 'can do' attitude, stay positive, believe in ourselves and achieve what we want to do in our lives. Going back to fight or flight we can choose to run or face our difficulties head on and drive through them with a positive attitude and built-in resolve to push through any obstacle that gets in our way and clouds our thinking and actions. I found that being tenacious and therefore to keep going is the key to getting through difficult periods of your life and avoid procrastination and stagnation which can only lead to despair.

As a Liverpool supporter for over 40 years, when the Kop sings you'll never walk alone, the hair stand on the back of your neck. This song and the philosophy behind it has taught me that anything is possible even under the most difficult and dark circumstances, to have the resilience and belief that anything is possible, that even through the darkest storms you can come out the other side and that you never walk alone.

Never more have I felt the need to dig deep and push through dark storms and find willpower and resilience than during my journey of completing my first ever marathon back in London Olympic year of 2012. Just five weeks before the start of the race, unfortunately in training, I developed a painful Achilles injury setback. The reality hit me that it was going to be extremely difficult to compete with such a short time to recover. However, after extensive physiotherapy and considerable testing ice baths and despite the last 12 miles the injury flared up again, I somehow managed to join the 1% club. This is the small amount of people in the world that have successfully completed this testing distance. The joy and relief of crossing the line, in having a silver recovery blanket draped over me and receiving my medal was amazing and an experience I will never forget. It was also the fundraising for a good cause close to my heart that kept me going. Life is like a marathon, it is not a sprint. You just have to keep going when life is tough; you need to find inner resilience and willpower when faced with difficult obstacles but through digging deep, I believe the human spirit is remarkable when faced with extreme testing circumstances.

Therefore, don't live in the past. "Now is the only time that matters. Stop wasting it dwelling in the past."

These are characteristics of someone who isn't willing to give up. Someone who isn't going to accept anything but success. Someone whose dictionary doesn't include the words—failure or giving up. These are some of the most captivating character traits one can possess.

It's true, some may take longer than others to bounce back. But, regardless of who you are, you can do it too. No matter what you've endured, no matter who hurt you, if you're motivated, you too can be resilient.

Everything you can imagine, it can all be yours. All you need is the mental focus, the drive, and the motivation. You too can be resilient to go get it. To everyone else, that is revolutionary. Here's why:

You Become a New You

Rather than crawling back in your hole and ignoring everything, you're able to go out and face challenges. You may feel that you have let yourself down, but that doesn't stop you because you're able to take that emotion and use it as a motivator for new success.

You're able to fall and bounce back higher than you ever have before. With that, you reinvent yourself mentally and emotionally. You become revolutionary, you raise questions in others, and you open new doors.

You See the Future

Everyone has issues they deal with whether it's personal, business, or maybe relationships. You don't deny them, but neither do you keep bringing them up.

You're able to put them aside and see the bright future ahead. Resilient beings aren't constantly wondering, *What if*, they're wondering, *Okay, now what's next?* It's a mind-set.

If you get laid off from a job, you focus on how much better the next job will be. How much more productive will you be in your new position? The past will never leave you, but it's not about the past, it's about the 'now' and what's next.

You Can Build Resistance

From your resilience, you become stronger. The new obstacles you face become less of a burden. There is nothing that will be able to knock you down, and people will realise that.

Nobody Must Hold You

Your bounce back will make you realise that you don't need others to console you. You are your own glue. In fact, after others seeing this change within you, they will change too.

You Learn How to Deal

At this point, you've realised how to deal with problems. After all, you're able to bounce back from the biggest one yet. You use your own formula to input a situation and output success.

Resilience is all about being able to overcome the unexpected. Sustainability is about survival. The goal of resilience is to thrive.

And as a wise person once said, "When we tackle obstacles, we find hidden reserves of courage and resilience we did not know we had. And it is only when we are faced with failure do we realise that these resources were always there within us. We only need to find them and move on with our lives."

Chapter 8
Maintaining Happiness 'The Self Concept'

We have all been sad. We have lost loves, dreams, pride, hopes, faith and on and on. Even periods of serious depression are not rare events. About 15% of us have been so depressed that it would have been wise to seek professional help (Wilcoxon, Schrader & Nelson, 1976).

But only one third of depressed people seek treatment. In the UK NHS statistics show that only 38% of men are referred to Individual Access to Psychological Therapies (IAPT) services with Wellbeing teams but sadly 78% of death from suicide are men. Significantly, 74% of women who have diagnosed depression have talked to someone about it but only 53% who are depressed have. This is significant as 90% of prisoners in the UK are men. 30% to 50% of rough sleepers have mental health problems and sadly 25% die from suicide. Even at School boys are 4 times more likely than girls to be diagnosed with behavioural emotional or social difficulties. So why is this? The obvious answer is that men clearly are struggling to talk about their feelings compared to women. But it's much more complex than that. The men I have spoken to at therapy sessions feel a sense of loss of identity and role within the modern world and struggling to find a balance from being strong a bread winner. Today the bread winner is now close to 50% equal in the role for men and women in a UK household as women are becoming more equal in the work place but still have the same issues as the '70s with lack of choice due to breaks in career from bringing up children.

Regarding the self-concept in which we develop sadness and happiness and a low or a high self-esteem from self-help books are vital.

Being depressed or anxious is the first or second most frequent reason why people are admitted to the psychiatric wards in general hospitals. A Commission on Mental Health estimated that 1 out of 4 of us (about 1 in 10 for males and 1 in 4 for females), will suffer from depression sometime in our lives. That is 20% in an affluent country the UK—one of the happiest country on earth with Finland being the happiest; what about the poor countries?

Women are twice as likely as men to be depressed; men get upset over jobs, women over relationships; married people in 'not very happy relationships' are more likely to be sad than unmarried and divorced people.

Depression is not only common, it can be very serious. In Western countries such as the UK, statistics have shown that sadly one person every minute attempts suicide; one person every 24 minutes succeeds. In the US alone, statistics have illustrated that shockingly there are more suicides than murders.

Edwin Shneidman, suicide prevention pioneer who died in 2009, developed his 10 commonalities study in 1959. This study was vital in showing common themes of the desperate and permanent need to end one's life and the need to be aware, which was most importantly the start of suicide prevention we use today.

Suicide is so sad because it is a permanent, desperate solution to a temporary problem. What a loss to the world that individuals kill themselves. What a blow to each family in which an unnecessary death occurs. However, I wish to focus not on clinical depression and suicide but feelings most of us have such as the following: depression, sadness, disappointment, loneliness, self-criticism, low self-concepts, guilt, shame, boredom, tiredness, lack of interests, lack of meaning in life, etc.

Overall, depression costs more in treatment and lost work than heart disease. Are some people just naturally happy? It sometimes seems like it. Were they just born with the hard wiring that makes them happy, cheerful, active, social, and optimistic?

Maybe. It might have been an inherited family trait, but happiness happens in other ways apparently. For instance, in many cases happy people are different from anyone else in the family; indeed, some had an unpleasant, neglectful, abusive family which they had trouble understanding but learned to tolerate.

The self-concept approach to happiness begins with the notion that your self-concept, or how you view yourself, is the key contributing factor to your happiness.

I have broken down the self-concept into two parts: identity and self-worth. Identity is further broken down into two components: "who you are" and "what you are". Both components also influence your feelings of self-worth.

Part of your self-concept deals with your identity, which includes "what you are" or in other words, what you do for a living. Part of the beauty of growing up in a developed nation is that we all have many choices regarding what we become, and hopefully our work provides us with some type of satisfaction.

The second part of your identity is "who you are" which includes your personality, character, and self-confidence level. Your personality is something you are born with, which forms during childhood and continues to grow as you mature throughout adolescence and adult life. Personality can be broken down into many traits—introverted versus extroverted, for example—and influences all your decisions in life.

Your character is shaped by your morals and values, which are further shaped by your socialisation into the society in which you live. Character, like your personality, is broken down into many components: integrity and compassion being two of the many. Your character determines many of your wants, hopes, and dreams, and how you will go about attaining them.

Although self-confidence is sometimes considered a personality trait, it is learnt and built from an early age by having positive experiences and achieving goals. Self-confidence, in my opinion, should never become egocentric; it is always best to remain level headed about what happens in life.

Your sources of self-worth are as individual to you as the personality you are born with. It is a by-product of your identity as well as the other choices you make pertaining to all aspects of your life. Self-worth is a difficult concept to grasp and may best be explained through an example: first, you have an individual who is unhappy with themselves and their life at present. This individual is introverted (personality), believes in doing the right thing (character), and has a low self-confidence level. Because this individual is introverted, he may pursue a career that does not involve interacting with the public and may obtain great satisfaction from knowing that his work contributes to the wellbeing of others.

Based on the self-concept theory, this individual will receive a sense of self-worth from the work he is doing, both because it suits his personality and is aligned with his morals—the increased self-worth will improve his self-confidence level.

Personality and character are about making choices in life and emergence of self-worth is a by-product of these choices. That's not to say that someone else's choices may be entirely different, and he may be equally as satisfied. Feelings of self-worth don't necessarily stem from your identity either. Your self-concept improves by your wants, hopes, and dreams occurring. Identity is what *influences* your wants, hopes, and dreams.

The first step in the self-concept approach to happiness is something every human being must do: meet his or her basic needs.

Basic needs include food, water, shelter, clothing, and sexual needs. Other than sexual needs, the first four require at least a subsistence level of income and for everyone to maximise his or her skills and talents in the workforce to meet their basic needs (and hopefully exceed those needs, so that they may focus part of their efforts on their wants).

I would like to introduce two topics to the discussion at this point: quality of life and inequality, the two topics that are interrelated. Unfortunately, in a developed society, some skills are valued higher than others; monetary worth of certain skill sets allows the quality of life to be greater for some individuals than others. This leads to inequality amongst the people living in these societies, which causes conflict between diverse groups of people, and leads some people to lead relatively unhappy lives. However, happiness is possible for everyone, regardless of property portfolio or career.

Life is all about focusing on the things you can control. Some things, like how someone treats you, for example, are better left not to worry about. Treating someone poorly is a character flaw of the person who chooses to live that way. And in a society, that places so much value on what one has, it is usually better not to compare yourself to other people.

The next step in the self-concept approach to happiness (after meeting your basic needs) is determining your wants.

Wants are influenced by your personality, character, and socialisation, and can constitute just about anything a person can imagine. It is important to note that wants should never victimise others. They are about what we ourselves can attain and achieve. Wants include possessions, relationships (both friendships and romantic interests), and experiences, along with just about anything else.

So, it is necessary to first think introspectively and do a self-inventory. You must discover what gives you feelings of self-worth—this depends upon your personality and character. Furthermore, you must think retrospectively and take a good, hard look at your life: the point is to look at social influences (upbringing, for example) and attempt to look beyond them and discover what is truly important to you. By focusing on what's truly important, you are better able to set goals whose attainment will contribute most positively to your view of yourself. After determining the things you want in life, you can begin to set goals for yourself.

Remember, it is always best to remain level headed and realistic. Following the goal-setting process, the next component in self-concept theory is expectations. Based on our wants, we all have expectations of whether these wants will materialise. These expectations exist on a continuum, ranging from very high to very low, and consists of everything in between these two extremes. Again, it is important to consider your identity and what is truly important to you when figuring out your expectations of an event occurring.

The role identity plays in determining expectations is that it helps us draw conclusions about what is possible for us to attain or achieve.

For example, if we are highly motivated by financial success and we have the skills to attain it, we may have higher expectations of attaining financial success.

Conversely, if we are less motivated by financial success, and more motivated by helping others, then our expectations of attaining financial success might me much lower, and our expectations of impacting the lives of others would be much higher. When considering what is truly important to you, your expectations of achievement or attainment of outcomes vary based on your degree of motivation and skill levels (which are influenced by your identity and sources of self-worth).

Expectations of events occurring are also influenced by social influence and past experiences. Social influences on expectations include upbringing, friends, family, the society in which we live, and media, literature, and popular culture.

First, your upbringing (in this case, the economic class in which you were born) and the careers of your parents probably play the largest role in determining your expectations.

For example, if you came from a middle-class family in which the primary breadwinner was a tradesman, not only would it be more likely that you'd become a tradesman yourself, but you would believe that this was attainable, and you would most likely have lofty expectations of living a middle-class life as an adult. I will comment that this concept is not universal; it is possible to have more than what your parents had, but it is the exception rather than the example.

Friends and family, although they care about you, have opinions and expectations about the choices you make. They will influence your choices and expectations, as much as you'd like for them not to. Media, literature, and popular culture also creates imprints on the human mind, again, however much you'd like for them not to. These imprints influence your wants and your expectations of these wants to materialise.

An example would be a popular hip-hop artist with a similar background to yours; this may increase your expectations that you too can become a rap artist, unlikely as it may be. Socialisation means learning and adopting the norms and values of a given society. Wealth attainment, for example, may appear more realistic in some societies than others.

Past experiences, any event you've already experienced, also factors into your expectations of wants to occur. Let's say you made the traveling team for a youth athletic program when you were young; during your young adult years, you may have higher expectations of playing that sport in college. On the other hand, if your goal was to be an actor and you didn't get a role in your high school play, your expectations of landing a professional acting role would be considerably low.

In sum, your expectations of positive or negative outcomes will be like what you've already experienced and depends on what has already happened in your life.

So far, I've discussed the self-concept: how self-concept and socialisation influences what you want and expectations of wants to occur, along with what influences your expectations of your wants materialising. The last piece to the self-concept theory deals with outcomes, whether your wants occur.

It is vital to understand that outcomes will have a positive or negative contribution on your self-concept. Desirable outcomes will have a positive contribution on your self-concept, while undesirable outcomes will have a negative. Knowing that *how you view* yourself is the key contributing factor to your happiness, the idea is to maximise desirable outcomes, while trying to eliminate as many undesirable ones as possible.

How much you want something and how important it is to you will impact both your motivation to attain it, and how much the outcome of that want occurring will positively or negatively contribute to your self-concept. If you really want to marry your girlfriend and she says yes to your proposal, this will significantly contribute positively to your self-concept. However, if she denies you, this may significantly contribute to it negatively and may even trigger depression.

To reiterate, lofty expectations of a want occurring along with undesirable outcomes have negative contributions on your self-concept.

Conversely, lower expectations of a want occurring, and desirable outcomes create positive contributions. Variable outcomes exist on a continuum and are directly related to positive or negative contributions to your self-concept.

In the end, happiness is how we view ourselves and deal with our experiences, both negative and positive.

It is vital to have a healthy positive self-concept. The self-concept is what is known in psychology how we feel and see ourselves in the world. In short, how happy or sad we are and linked to our self-esteem and confidence.

The self-concept can also be a negative dark place where we can feel sad perhaps lonely and even depressed and carry our self-destructive behaviour that feeds our negative distorted thinking. To keep this simple we have a choice of what self-concept we have and vitally choosing to be happy with great self-worth and confidence or sad and miserable.

The good news is that if we have a negative self-concept we can change to be happier and lead fulfilling lives. This can be achieved by simply changing our dominant thoughts and thinking. One of the most important quotes I ever heard that completely changed my life was this.

"Changing our thinking and change your life."

Chapter 9
The Mental Laws 'Attraction, Belief and Expectation'

"Your mental energy travels at the speed of light. It travels and is so fine that it goes through any substance. You can think a thought here and it can connect with someone on the other side of the world."

"Your mind is incredibly powerful, but it is a neutral law. If you think negative thoughts, you will attract negative things into your life as well."

This is what *The Secret* is based on, The Law of Attraction, however, they missed a critical point in that movie; work, it takes challenging work to be successful along with thinking in the right manner.

"The more emotion that is attached to a thought, the greater is the intensity of the vibration. Everything radiates outward."

And we engage in sympathetic resonance, where we resonate with other people, we resonate with ideas, we resonate with conversations, we resonate with subjects that we like to study and learn about.

We have this all the time and that is The Law of Attraction, it means: "It's something within you is resonating within something outside of you."

"If you want to be really successful and you see successful people and you start to resonate with their accomplishments, you start to become more like them."

"Now here's a crucial point people don't realise, this also explains what is called The Law of Repulsion, if you hold a negative thought you repel anything associated with that thought out of your life, so many people are brought up to look down on those who are successful, to criticise successful people. This is fatal because if you criticise successful people even in your heart it drives success out of your life, it guarantees you'll never accomplish anything with your life, you'll always be miserable and unsuccessful."

"And therefore, it's so important for you to admire people who are enjoying the success that you desire. Admire successful, happy people and you will create this sympathetic resonance and you begin to attract into your life the people, ideas, and circumstances that will enable you to be like one of those people."

"Your expectations, especially about your outcomes, become your own self-fulfilling prophecies. If you expect something to happen, it usually happens. If you expect it to happen, you'll act consistent with it happening."

"When you expect to be successful, it totally transforms your attitude and your results. You can manufacture your own expectations. Whatever you expect with confidence becomes your own self-fulfilling prophecy."

So, cast your net think big and catch your lofty expectations beliefs and attract people who desire your beliefs expectations and values.

"The greatest of all attitudes, the catalyst that causes your potential to unlock like a chemical catalyst, that causes an explosive effect is confident expectations, an attitude of confident expectation transforms your attitude towards your world. Always expect the best. Repeat this throughout the day, start your day with this affirmation: I believe that something wonderful is going to happen to me today."

"The Law of Belief. Whatever you believe with feeling becomes your reality. Whatever you believe with feeling, with emotion, with intensity, it becomes your reality because you always act based on your beliefs, and the more intensely you hold the belief the more the belief becomes true for you."

"The turning point in many people's lives is when they challenge old beliefs that they are meant to be working individuals. There are two sets of beliefs, conscious and unconscious beliefs. It isn't what hurts us, it's what we know that isn't true. Many things we know about ourselves is not true at all."

"People develop Scotomas (Blind Spots). Once we've decided to believe certain things we do not see anything that contradicts it. Your biggest obstacle is usually self-limiting beliefs. We have obstacles within our mind that we create. You must have an unshakeable belief that you will succeed." ('Scotomas' 2013 Retina Fifth Edition and handbook of clinical Neurology 2011)

I've always found that anything worth achieving will always have obstacles in the way and you've got to have that drive and determination to overcome those obstacles on route to whatever it is that you want to accomplish. A technique I use to help people improve their self-esteem is called mirroring. Try saying positive affirmations at the mirror. The best time to practice this is first thing in the morning and last thing at night. The morning sets you up with positive belief in yourself while at night, you go to bed thinking positive thoughts.

With the mental Laws of Belief, Expectation and Attraction, it's important that you believe with conviction. So back to mirroring and say the following positive affirmations.

I believe something truly amazing will happen to me today.

I expect good things will happen to me today.

I expect abundance of good people to come into my life.

Then stand back and watch the universe in action in all its wonder work for you. Watch in amazement as suddenly good things happen for you. Doors open and unexpected life-changing events occur for you. The Law of Belief, Expectation and Attraction brought my future wife like an angel from heaven to me, so try it, and these positive affirmations will work for you too.

Chapter 10
Goals Are Not Goals Unless They Are Written Down

Top-level athletes, successful business-people and achievers in all fields all set goals. Setting goals gives you long term vision and short-term motivation. It focuses your acquisition of knowledge, and helps you to organise your time and your resources so that you can make the very most of your life. Goals help us believe in ourselves. Setting goals for yourself is a way to fuel your ambition. Goal setting isn't about creating a plan for life and holding yourself accountable, it's also about giving us the inspiration necessary to aim for things we never thought were possible.

Goals are what take us forward in life; they are the oxygen to our dreams. They are the first steps to every journey we take and are also our last. It's important that you realise the significance and importance of goal-setting and apply this knowledge in your life. Setting goals in life is the most important action you can take, because you are holding yourself accountable for the results.

"The trouble with not having a goal is that you can spend your life running up and down a field and never score." Bill Copeland.

"You need a plan to build a house. To build a life, it is even more important to have a plan or goal." Zig Ziglar.

Do you set goals for yourself? What are the goals for the next year? How about 3 to 5 years? 10 years and so on. What are your aspirations for life? You need a plan to build a house.

Goal setting is the first step to successful achievement. It marks your first point towards success.

Here are 8 reasons why it is important to set goals:

1. To take control of your life and avoid sleepwalking through life. Even through challenging work, people don't feel like you're getting what you want. This is because the direction of where the people want to go and what they wish to achieve isn't clear. Students graduate and don't have a sense of direction of what they want to do with their lives, hence, they sleep walk. They simply did not teach this stuff in our UK and Western Schools of 'how to be a success'. As Bill Copeland said when you don't set goals you can spend your life running up and down and not achieving anything significant that makes a difference to the quality of your life. To achieve success top performers always set goals and make plans on how to achieve them. They also write it down because without writing it down it's not really a goal just wish-full thinking and hope with no structure and plan. When you have vision, you look forward not backwards from the past but at your future and all its possibilities. You ensure that you are not resting on your laurels and pushing forward with your life to get the best results and achievements possible rather than waiting for things to happen. As well as writing them down its important they are measurable and enable improvement. It is vital to set specific targets and milestones and at the same time allow you to work towards working hard to achieve. It also makes you passionate about life and stay motivated and focused. Most importantly goals enable you to have sense of purpose in life and because you feel you have direction keep you happy, see chapter 7 on maintaining happiness. It will allow you to, as famously quoted in the book 'Ask for the moon and end up at the stars', to achieving realistic

goals. If you don't try to aim big, then you won't achieve big or somewhere in-between. Goals also give a vision it is your mission statement about what you want to achieve and how you are going to achieve it.

2. At the same time by setting a clear 3 to 5-year plan shows you value yourself and that you deserve to attract people and circumstances in your life, your focus goal setting and challenging work should achieve. It is important you know that all things are created first in the mind and then in the physical world. In other words, everything has cause and effect and the consequences from your actions such as goal setting will reap high rewards of success.

3. Gives life purpose and general direction. Your goals give you focus and most importantly give you positive energy to achieve.

4. Creates accountability and avoid blaming as you are in charge and control of your destiny and the failure or success you achieve. By setting specific targets, you can easily see if you are on track and if not adjust the plan to achieve the goals. I set daily, weekly, monthly goals and by setting a clear plan of how to achieve simply achieve them with time to spare.

5. In short setting goals motivates you like nothing else. When you connect yourself with your goals you connect yourself with your desires, see chapter 4 on we desire what we can't have. Yes, you can but only if you set clear goals and make clear plans for your future and how to achieve them. Goals motivate you to strive to be better and a success in whatever you choose to do yes choose because it's about taking control of your destiny. This is especially vital to set goals if you are not in a good place or even depressed. It is a powerful tool and enables you despite planning your future to live in moment for the moment and enjoy life and lead a more fulfilling life. It reminds you of your passions and love and what you enjoy

about life and what makes you happy and enables us to think positively about any negative obstacles that we might find with our goals and plans. To quote Henry Ford once famously said, "Obstacles are those things you see when you take your eyes off the goal." I believe from my therapy sessions that when you are feeling negative or down, it's often because there is no focus and most vital nothing to look forward to in your life. Your goals are like rainbows to strive for to push through the dark clouds and storm. Even if you lose motivation which of course happens to all of us even the best performers, goals enable you to redirect and build resilience to negative obstacles because they make you think more clearly and creatively and maintain happiness and balance in your life.

6. Goals also enable you to move forward from comfort Zone mentality which stunts personal development. It makes you think you can do it. "I can be the best." I *can* attitude. It makes you maximise your unique potential as a human being to be the best you can become. These targets make you venture out into the unknown and take risks and not follow the crowd and be different, see chapter 6 on the importance of being different and thinking out of the box. These targets make you venture into unfamiliar places and new situations that put you automatically in the growth mode. They make you stretch beyond your normal self and reach new heights. For example, setting a time limit for your run lets you know if you should be running faster. Setting weight loss targets helps you to know if your actions have been effective in losing weight.

7. Setting a career goal ensures that you are not settling for anything less than what you desire.

Live your best life. Finally, goals ensure that you get the best out of life. Whether you want this or not, time will pass in your life. It is vital to think that if you don't make a five-year plan in 5 years you are 5 years older and no further forward in your life.

8. Goals with specific measures and deadlines that you are maximising your experience on earth. If you already have discovered your life purpose, your goals will help you get the best out of your purpose for life. Imagine the world is your oyster. There are millions, billions of things you can encounter.

There are endless possibilities of what you can accomplish. What if you can do whatever you want? What do you want to achieve? What do you want to see, do and experience in your life? Set goals, make them happen, and watch as you create your best. Start setting goals.

Ask yourself this: What are my goals for 1, 3, 5 years or 10? If you just take some time out to set your goals now. I guarantee you will experience more growth as a person. By just spending a few minutes to articulate some aspirations that you have in mind to achieve you will experience more progress in your life a year from now than if you don't set goals or have a life plan.

It's almost 80 years since an Englishman Alec Mace came up with the idea of goal-setting as a way of getting people to live more fulfilling lives. Here is a history of goal setting facts and figures. If you don't write your goals down, they are only hopes and dreams and not true achievable goals. By writing your goals down you are making a clear plan to achieve something big or small. Without writing it down its more wishful thinking with no clear direction of how to achieve it. However, as you are writing down your goals it already makes it more achievable or you are setting yourself up to fail. *SMART* principles were developed and used in business and are an effective way not just in business but setting everyday realistic goals that are achievable. However, don't be a perfectionist because you are also setting yourself up to fail.

Goals need to be realistic and achievable otherwise you could fail in your life. Once you have a planned project, turn your attention to developing several goals that will enable you to be successful. Goals should be SMART—Specific, measurable, agreed upon, realistic, and time based.

Specific—significant, stretching
Measurable—meaningful, motivational
Achievable—agreed upon, attainable, acceptable
Realistic—relevant, reasonable and rewarding
Time Based—trackable, timely and tangible.

To Quote renowned American Philosopher and writer Elbert Hubbard: "Many people fail in life, not for lack of ability or brains or even courage, but simply because they have never organised their energies around a goal."

When setting goals, ask yourself the ultimate question. If you win the National Lottery tomorrow, what would you do regarding your career, relationships and purpose in life? If you decide to leave your job, you are in the wrong career. So don't wait to win the lottery, do something about it now. What motivates and stimulates you to give you a sense of meaning and purpose in your life? This is what psychologists call 'drivers'. So what 'drives' you to get up in the morning? If your lottery question still involves your career and relationship, then congratulations, you are likely to be feeling peace of mind, content and fulfilled in your life. You are on a journey, have a clear plan and have set goals that have made a difference in your life.

Most importantly when setting any goals, realise it's not all about you, make them about others. This makes a real difference both to your life and the lives of others. In short, set ethical and spiritual goals which give something back and feel good when doing them. It's not all about money as some self-help books would have you believe; this does not make you happy. This is more about doing something with your life that makes a difference and gives you satisfaction and perhaps a sense of wonderment of what you can achieve, which is part of what makes us unique human beings who are capable of doing amazing and exciting things with our lives, the world and the universe we live in today and will be living in the future.

Chapter 11
Laugh and Success Will Smile on You

You will become a magnet to positive things happening in your life. Remember the law of attraction, laughter and smiling will create confidence, improve your self-concept and at the same time self-esteem and attract people and circumstances which have the same core beliefs and expectations as you. In short, you will attract positive people. This is important for professional relationships, work career as well as attracting positive romantic relationships who share your positive beliefs and zest for life. Most importantly, the law of attraction can also attract negative people who will drain you of energy, so what do you want? It's amazing how much laughing and smiling is good for the soul and most vitally improve your mental and physical wellbeing. Studies have shown that staying positive having resilience and a positive mind can enable people to avoid negative relationships and even serious mental conditions such as depression and anxiety. As a therapist, I have found that Cognitive Behavioural Therapy CBT works for this kind of distorted thinking, but you can do a few simple things to prevent the need for this kind of therapy with laughter and smiling and staying positive is a very powerful tool to attracting the right kind of mate and success in your life. If we're destroying our trees and destroying our environment and hurting animals and hurting one another and all that stuff, there's got to be a very powerful energy to fight that. I think we need more love in the world. We need more kindness, more compassion, more joy and more laughter. I want to contribute to that. Laughter is something that everyone has experienced or encountered at some point in their life.

Whether it was while watching TV, talking with people, listening to a joke or a spur of the moment thing, we all know the great feeling that comes from laughter; mainly because it is a natural reaction in response to a stimulus that is very hard to control. But how is laughter the key to happiness, you might ask?

For one thing, laughter can lift your spirits and put you in a positive mood. Whether you are feeling down or upset about something, we all know that, regardless of what the circumstance is, if we see something that makes us laugh we start to feel better. We often tend to rely on laughter during the rough patches in our life because it makes us feel good and helps cheer us up. It is for this reason that we may start to laugh or giggle during a serious situation or moment.

Aside from making us feel good and better emotionally, laughter has been scientifically proven to help keep us healthy.

Laughter has the capability to strengthen the immune system, lower blood sugar, enhance blood flow and circulation, as well as reduce stress caused by burdens and conflicts. When we experience physical pain, laughter helps ease the pain and acts a temporary 'medicine.'

Personally, a time when I found out the significant impact of laughter was when I was sick and in pain. It helped make me forget about how much I was hurting and lifted my spirits to the point where I became happy despite the circumstances.

However, one of the most important reasons we laugh, is simply because it is contagious. We have all experienced it.
One person laughs at a silly thing, and then everyone starts laughing. In most cases, the contagious laugh is no longer directed at the funny thing or situation, but the person's laugh who started the laughing.

One of the best feelings is laughing uncontrollably, because it allows us to live in the moment and briefly forget about all the other commotion going on in our lives. Laughter helps us remain happy in life, because without a laugh here and there, life can get very boring.

When we laugh we can appreciate the trivial things life must offer, and the little comments, acts or moments that make us feel happy and liberated.

Laughter can be thought of as a universal language. Everyone can do it, everyone can use it, and everyone can understand it, regardless of gender, race, ethnicity or religion. It's something that doesn't separate us from others—instead it brings people together. Therefore, next time you hear or see something worth laughing about, don't be hesitant—do it. Not only does it help you stay healthy, but overall it makes you feel good about yourself, and it is the ultimate key to happiness in life.

There is even laughter therapy and laughter yoga so clearly laughter is becoming recognised as to how important it is to smile and laugh which makes us feel and display happiness. It also helps us live longer as studies have shown happy people live longer healthier lives than those sad and depressed people. People also live longer if they can do the things they want to do need to do and like doing. Everyone has vices in life such as chocolate and or eating too much food they enjoy but as long as they are happy, the Chinese proverb said when trying a new experience "what does not hurt you will not affect you" stands up well. Although I totally condone drinking and smoking and have witnessed the devastating effects, you often here stories of people drinking and smoking like a trouper and living to 100.

The only explanation I can provide is they were happy and laughed and enjoyed life and lived life to the maximum which prevented heart disease and strain and stress on vital organs from not being unhappy and depressed.

As well as no action stopping Wars humour has as well. A famous quote in a famous war said, "We need to cut costs, sir, and need to reduce our army down from 3000 to 1000 men."

In which the Connell replied, "I will agree to this only if the enemy agree to reduce their army down to 1000 men." With this response, there was a roar of laughter on the board and of course no reductions were made, and it was probably the reason we won that famous war.

Chapter 12
Count Your Blessings and Go Back to Nature

It's so important to not forget, when things are going wrong that we forget what is going right in our lives. It is amazing if we use this powerful mental tool and change our thinking to just counting our blessings for all that is good in our lives can be as simple as being mindful and going back to nature.

Going back to nature gives us peace of mind in the world and lets us just be and relax which aids our mental health and maintains happiness. As Johnson once said, "Life just is, go with the flow, live life for the moment let it happen." It is vital for all our wellbeing that we count our blessings and have peace of mind and tranquillity.

This will enable us to maintain a healthy balance, healthy life style keeps physically well at the same time as holistically keeping us mentally stable and fit. This can only be a good thing. An effective way to maintain peace of mind is through mindfulness, meditation and yoga. Gratitude is an emotion expressing appreciation for what one has—as opposed to, for example, a consumer-driven emphasis on what one wants. Gratitude is getting a great deal of attention as a facet of positive psychology: Studies show that we can deliberately cultivate gratitude, and can increase our well-being and happiness by doing so.

Gratitude makes us happier. That's what many spiritual traditions maintain. Now scientific research backs such claims. And that's what we can easily observe in our own life and that of others.

"I've realised that I can change mind channels."

"You sound like a TV remote!"

"It's a bit like that. I can switch from negative thoughts to positive ones."

"And what kind of thoughts do you switch to?"

"Thoughts about being grateful for the good things in my life. That's made me happier."

Scientist have found that grateful people

1. Show higher levels of positive emotions, life satisfaction, vitality, and optimism.
2. Experience lower levels of depression and stress.
3. Have more capacity for compassion.
4. Are rated as more generous and helpful by other people.
5. Are more likely to have a spiritual practice.
6. Place less importance on materialism.
7. Are more likely to make progress towards important personal goals.
8. Exercise more regularly, report fewer physical symptoms, and feel healthier.

Here are 5 powerful gratitude exercises:

1. Keep a Gratitude Diary

Write down everything you are grateful for at least once a week. According to research those who kept gratitude diaries on a weekly basis exercise more regularly, report fewer physical symptoms, feel better about their lives, and are more optimistic about the upcoming week compared to those who record hassles or neutral life events. They are also more likely to make progress towards important personal goals.

2. Count Your Blessings

Before you fall asleep, reflect on the day and identify 5 things you are grateful for. According to Prof Emmons, a group of young adults who did a daily gratitude exercise showed higher levels of positive states of alertness, enthusiasm, determination, attentiveness and energy compared to those participants who focussed on hassles or negative comparisons.

3. Tell Your Friends and Others That You Are Grateful to Them

In his book *Authentic Happiness*, Prof Martin Seligman suggests a powerful way of practising gratitude:

Choose an important person in your past to whom you have never fully expressed your thanks.

Meet with the person face to face and read out the testimonial.

When reflecting on this exercise it occurred to me that some people to whom I am grateful to are dead. So, what I did was to write the testimonial page, go to a secluded bend in the river, read the page aloud and then offer it to the waters. That was very powerful for me!

4. See adversity as an opportunity to learn and grow

We knew all about this when we were toddlers! We would fall and get up, fall and get up—and it was all part of learning to walk. It's important to remind ourselves that falling is an integral part of learning.

5. Change from Negative to Positive Thoughts

In CBT there is a simple method to enable people to dwell on positive thoughts, instead of on negative issues. Either by carrying a clicker pen or elastic band around with them. Whenever people notice they are dwelling on negative issues, they are asked to click the pen or ping the elastic band. This acts as a trigger to change one's 'thought channel'.

I tried it and it works! For sure it's a great skill to be able to change our thoughts. At the same time, I sometimes wonder whether the relentless emphasis on 'positive' thoughts impoverishes our life. After all, to yearn, to grieve, or to doubt—that too means to be human. What do you think?

If you want to see whether these 'gratitude interventions' make you happier, you can take a test to see how happy you are before trying them out. (This is the General Happiness Scale according to proof Martin Seligman). Then repeat the test two weeks later and see if there is any change.

What is your experience of gratitude?

There are plenty of theories and tools used in CBT such as mood diaries which are negative such as anxiety and depression mood diaries and emotional scales, but I have turned it on its head and thinking differently remember chapter 6 and have come up with gratitude theory which I have incorporated into an actual therapy. 'Gratitude therapy' which uses some ideas from Seligman but focuses on missing out all the active person centred listening techniques. In short, a client coming with a presenting issue such as depression caused by external event of a breakdown of relationship, you simply ignore all the negative part and just concentrate on 20 questions I have designed called *GRATS*. My GRAT questionnaire is 1 to 20. For example, name one thing that is going well in your life now? Rather than the negative opposite terrible things happening. I believe by ignoring and not recognising the negative automatic thoughts such as used in CBT and *REBT* and keeping the cognitive brain positive and only focusing on positive transforms the thoughts in only being of gratitude and positivity which helps the client learn to develop and recognise that there are good things in their life. This make it worth living and fighting for and not concentrating on negativity which causes unhappiness and health issues. In roles previously for recovery and wellbeing, wellbeing, wellness action plans or Wellness Recovery Action Plans *WRAPS* are used as a wellness tool box to recognise triggers and when a person is in a crisis putting a plan of prevention together. However, these WRAPS are usually in the form of a work book and don't really come alive and toolboxes that you can pick up objects such as photographs of memories and loved ones are more meaningful to prevent relapse than written down which my experience of working with people with mental health, see as an added anxiety that its paperwork. With the GRATS idea you simply bypass all negativity and just focus on the here and now what currently is going well in your life not the presenting issue from the past. For example, a question I often use is as follows, what are you grateful for in your life? By framing the question with a positive bias will result in a positive response and usually they will focus on something that is good happening despite all the negativity. Another example is what do you want to change in your life to make you grateful of what you have? Although a slight negative bias it often results in reflective thinking and goal setting and planning to achieve it. I will be discussing this in detail in my next book my whole gratitude therapy and theories but just want to give you a taste to what can be achieved by changing your thinking and transforming your life.

Chapter 13
Life Is a Miracle, Don't Waste It

I only must look at a busy roundabout to see what a 100 mile an hour life style we lead today. All going somewhere fast not with any thought for the next person in a car. All following the crowd remember chapter 6, the importance of being different and breaking away from this continuous cycle. Just be mindful even for one minute and take time to have a look and breath and smell nature and then realise at that point you can change not just follow the heard of sheep and do something amazing with your life as, 'Life is a miracle so don't waist it.' Stuck in traffic on your way to work. You're sitting in traffic just to get to work to sit in another meaningless meeting. Your boss doesn't respect you and you certainly don't respect him, but you have been faithfully towing the company line—smiling through the endless memos, company bureaucracy, late nights, etc.

What's the point of all of it, really? Job security? It's hard to call something secure when the company can fire you at will, any day or lay off 25% of its workforce next month. You may have loyalty to your company, but then in an instant, you realise your company is loyal only to its bottom line.

If you fantasise about quitting your job and becoming your own boss, you're not alone. What could be better than taking matters into your own hands, setting your own hours, and pursuing your own goals? You don't have to deal with rush-hour traffic, cubicle mazes, or mid-management bosses.

Certainly, starting a business is challenging work. It typically involves long days. But there's one major difference:

you will be putting all your time, creativity, and effort towards fulfilling your own dream, not someone else's.

It is important to remember that life is not a dress rehearsal, and that none of us should waste our time on doing things that don't spark fires within us.

Globally, we have seen countless examples where entrepreneurship helps lift men and women, families, and whole communities out of poverty. I was made redundant and suddenly had to be robust and come up with a new concept of making money and maintaining happiness.

With only a few qualification's and leaving school early and living on a council estate I found education late in life and after studying several Degrees, Diplomas and professional qualifications, I qualified as a psychotherapist and have never looked back. My main reason was I saw the benefits of therapy and secondly, I needed to urgently make a living in my life to support my family. Starting MB Counselling services and going alone was the best decision I ever made. I am now contented and fulfilled in my work as it involves helping people and improving the quality of their lives. Helping people is something I have always wanted to do at an early age and I think showed early promise as a young boy helping elderly people as a scout. The scout movement taught me a lot about team work and helping others. I have also met a likeminded person my wife who as a nurse specialist also helps many people. You will read about the importance of meeting likeminded people in chapter 16.

If you are thinking about becoming an entrepreneur or setting up your own business, here are eight lessons that I have learnt over the years:

1. Despite my situation the main goal shouldn't be to make lots of money or create an empire. A true entrepreneur's mission is to add value to the world and

make a meaningful change to people's lives; money and jobs are just the by-products.

2. If you are afraid of failing, you'll never get past the starting gate. An entrepreneur rides every wave, embraces every crash, and never lets the fear of striking out cause them to quit the game. All my past failures have paved the way for each of my current successes.

3. You need to follow your instincts. At times, this can mean giving the finger (and you know which one) to anyone who stands in your way.

4. Entrepreneurship is not about following the rules. Yes, I want my children to be respectful of others and give 100 percent in school, but I'm proudest when they colour outside the lines.

5. For a true entrepreneur, obstacles are just bumps in the road; they are never the end of the road.

6. Entrepreneurs never wait for things to be handed to them. There's never a 'perfect' time or opportunity, so stop waiting for one. You'll never get what you don't ask for or work for.

7. The most important rule when it comes to employees, customers and partners is to be genuine and kind. Everything else will fall into place.

8. As Richard Branson said, life isn't a dress rehearsal. And it is way too short to spend time following someone else's path or passions. Get out there, follow your dreams, and make the world a better place.

Are you happy and doing what you love every day and if not, isn't it time your pursued your entrepreneurial dreams?

It is a miracle that from birth we come into the world with the desire to discover and learn only to let our self-concept and attitude wreck our path to success. We are only here a very short-period of time. Time is precious. "Time is your most important asset."

"Prioritise how you spend it."

Therefore, it is a shame that we allow obstacles to distract us from our goals if we choose to not change.

This causes destructive thinking patterns and a cycle hard to break out of. We get more entrenched and later due to unhappiness and sense of learnt helplessness we can develop depression and anxiety. This causes a cycle of self-destructive behaviour, all this can be changed through realisation that this is not a dress rehearsal and the real thing, so no second chance if we choose not to change our ways. In short, we cannot change the past, but we can change our future of what time we have left on the planet to make amends and lead a fulfilling happy life from now on.

Life may not always fall into neat chapters, and you may not always get the satisfying ending you're looking for, but sometimes a good explanation is all the rewrite you need and do something different. Chapter 6 takes a chance and think out of the box. There are opportunities out there all you need is niche in the market, a new idea, belief, expectation and attract (the mental Laws Chap 9) people who share your beliefs and you will succeed.

Chapter 14
Give and Karma Will Give It Back from the Universe

Studies in mental health show that by giving helps improve depression and anxiety. This is because when you give something like a birthday or Christmas present or romantic gift it automatically increases endorphins, the feel-good factor hormones that make you feel good when you see the pleasure you give to others. This is also true in becoming a volunteer. Today in mental health there is the idea of peer mentoring where people with lived experience give to each other through being volunteers and peer mentors. It's not a coincidence that philanthropist's in Victorian times existed. They may have felt guilt too of their wealth but at the same time *giving* made them feel better. Concern for others is central to teachings of Sikhism as illustrated by the story of Guru. Giving to the hungry is seen as giving to God and genuinely from the human heart. A key principle of giving in Sikh religion is the idea of 'Sewa' which is the idea of mass equality which involves everyone sitting on the floor, so they are treated equally, and people give up time, talents and energy to serve others for the good of the community. Sikhism requires service to Waheguru (God), to Khalsa and to all of humanity.

We all know about good and bad karma. When you give something, like money, kindness, looking after someone, the universe gives it back to you. The vital component is you don't do it to gain anything you do it because you want to. Therefore, being armed with this knowledge why don't you try it. It's amazing how suddenly wonderful things, opportunities are given back to you from the universe if you apply this simple rule. Everybody wants to be happy and free from problems— they are our two basic wishes.

An example of 'giving and the universe will give back' can be illustrated through a feel-good factor story that happened to me recently. I lost my wedding ring at sea whilst swimming with my family in deep water at high tide at Shoreham Beach. Whilst I was devastated, what happened next was simply amazing and ended up on the front page of the *Argus*. The whole community, including a 7-year-old boy with a toy metal detector, pedestrians, cyclists, families and dog walkers all rallied around to find it after a social media campaign. Finally, after a long search another hero with a metal detector pulled off the impossible and found it. People have since told me they lost rings and never got them back. I believe this impossible miracle is a good example of 'when you do good you get it back from the universe'.

However, due to lacking wisdom or understanding karma, we mistakenly identify their actual causes and thus remain trapped in a cycle of pain and dissatisfaction.

By applying Buddha's teachings on Karma and the mind we can discover the 'key' to our own happiness and unlock our own potential for permanent freedom. Give and the universe will give it back.

There is no Karma, because time does not exist.

The Present, Past and Future are 'Simultaneously Occurring'. So, if there is no such thing as Karma, why do terrible things happen in one's life?

First, Let Me Define Karma:

Karma is the law of moral causation. The theory of Karma is a fundamental doctrine in Buddhism. This belief was prevalent in India before the advent of the Buddha.

Nevertheless, it was the Buddha who explained and formulated this doctrine in the complete form in which we have it today.

In this world, nothing happens to a person that he does not for some reason or other deserve. Usually, men of ordinary intellect cannot comprehend the actual reason or reasons. The definite invisible cause or causes of the visible effect is not necessarily confined to the present life, they may be traced to a proximate or remote past birth.

According to Buddhism, this inequality is due not only to heredity, environment, 'nature and nurture', but also to Karma. In other words, it is the result of our own past actions and our own present doings. We ourselves are responsible for our own happiness and misery. We create our own Heaven. We create our own Hell. We are the architects of our own fate. Perplexed by the seemingly inexplicable, apparent disparity that existed among humanity, a young truth-seeker approached the Buddha and questioned him regarding this intricate problem of inequality: "What is the cause, what is the reason, O Lord," questioned he, "that we find amongst mankind the short-lived and long-lived, the healthy and the diseased, the ugly and beautiful, those lacking influence and the powerful, the poor and the rich, the low-born and the high-born, and the ignorant and the wise?"

The Buddha's reply was:
"All living beings have actions (Karma) as their own, their inheritance, their congenital cause, their kinsman, their refuge. It is Karma that differentiates beings into low and high states."

If you do not like *your current past story*—take a new road in your mind. This will simultaneously change your Present, Past and Future. The 'present moment' is our point of power to turn any circumstance around, by creating again in our mind a new direction.

I love this mantra, from a terrific book, *Busting Loose from The Money Game* by Robert Steinfeld. I might be in the middle of an argument, and I say in my head, *I am the power and presents of God creating this. It is not real but completely made up. I choose for it to show up like this.*

Then I just stand there in silence, until the event shifts. It always works, like magic! When this happens it's so exciting to me, the other person changes too. Try it.

As, you evolve you can add or change any of the words in the mantra. For example, you can replace the word God, if you don't believe in a God. You could believe God is '*All That Is*' or a group of '*Avatars*', called the speakers, who have learnt to create at levels we cannot yet grasp. Either way, what you believe will become your reality. I have used the word 'God' even though I do not believe in one central deity, controlling mankind. Yet, in my early upbringing I was taught to pray to God, so this still resonates with me. As I evolve more, I am sure my taught beliefs will naturally change.

Karma cannot exist in the way we think of it, that we do something bad and we pay for it. The paying for what we feel we have done wrong is coming from 'our own hand'. *The judge and jury of our life is the voice in our head.* And the voice in our head hears different things depending on which lifetime that voice is experiencing. There is a Higher Self, overseeing all these voices, which gurus call, 'Enlightened One'. Validation of this comes from our intuitions, dreams or insights from our higher self.

Karma is self-imposed. We are the hardest judges on *OUR SELF*. No one would judge us harder than we judge ourselves. Therefore, the system of being allowed to create our own reality is so divine. It seems to have checks and balances because somewhere inside us, we decide if what we created is of merit. If either feels good or it does not. We create and interact with our creations and from these we learn to create better events and interactions. There is no divine punishment, and we do not have to punish ourselves for our mistakes in creations. We can just learn from them, laugh and create again better results. This is the key to happiness. Loving yourself unconditionally. It starts here, because you cannot love anything else until you love yourself.

Karma is only self-punishment based on what we feel we deserve.

If we think we did something bad, we may want to punish ourselves for several lifetimes, always by our own hand. If you think you might have done this because you are having a tough time with this life, go back in your mind to the past and create new past lives, ones where you did kind loving things, to yourself and those versions of you love in this life as if they have been time travellers in many life times. This will stop the subconscious negative cycle, and bring you back into your true being of joy.

We can give up this idea of Karma and save several lifetimes of misery, by learning to forgive the self all the time, its short comings. The punishments afflicted on us is from the 'ego'. The ego is created by the experiences of this lifetime, and uses these to navigate. But, you must raise above the voice in your head to remember you are creating your every event you are experiencing. The ego says, "Woe is me." It is not your higher self, knowing it creates everything you are experiencing.

If you are new to owning your creations, you can ask your higher self to create your ideal day. Appreciate the good and the bad will slowly disappear. There are people on earth, who have created an entire lifetime of great days, it is possible. When these people have a dreadful day, they are quick to get back up and focus better. Focus and the current moment are the key to ideal creations.

Chapter 15
The Quality of Our Relationships Defines Us

So how do we measure success? Most people wrongly measure it by materialist means such as income, possessions but for me, it is the quality of your relationships that really states how successful a human being you are. Let's take scrooge, was he happy as a miser with all his gold coins? No, of course he wasn't; he was miserable and most importantly alone in the world wallowing in his own misery and sadness. Therefore, I believe money does not automatically make you happy but who you share your life experiences with that really matters. As a therapist, I have worked with all kinds of people, some extremely poor with serious issues and health problems but significantly also millionaires who you would think should have no problems in the world having all that money.

"Material wealth is not real wealth."

"Materiel wealth won't make you a better or a happy person."

Remember the law of attraction! It reminds me of a couple I worked with in a residential home in the south of England. The couple both in their '80s had been married for 56 years but sadly did not know that they were still married or let alone that they knew each other or that they ever had a connection with each other. So many memories and life experiences they must have had together, why? Dementia is a debilitating condition that strips away cognition and most importantly memory. In the residential home, staff tried to re-connect them through photos and by trying to put them together at meal times but still no connection or triggering memory, not even with pictures. As soon as any kind of memory was briefly rekindled, they were instantly forgotten as the dementia was so severe, affecting the working short-term memory and long-term memory.

I am sure you could imagine the staff were very upset and desperate to find a solution. However, as further years went by the couple found they got on well together and had a lot in common and started playing cards together and sitting at meal times with each other and reminiscing talking about holidays and where they had been, still with no idea that they spent their entire life together to the point they started to fall in love together all over again. They wanted to get married. The staff showed them the marriage certificate which was forgotten in an instant like Groundhog Day. So, a mock wedding was set up and even though it was forgotten again in an instant for that moment they knew they were in love. Never underestimate the power of the law of attraction, the universe will draw two people together like a magnet. If you are meant to be together, nothing will separate you, not even a terrible debilitating condition.

Relationships are the most important aspects of our lives, yet we can often forget just how crucial our connections with other people are for our physical and mental wellbeing. People who are more socially connected to the family, friends or the community are happier, physically healthier and live longer, with fewer mental health problems than people who are less well connected. It's not just the number of friends you have or fake Facebook friends, you have or not but whether you're in a committed relationship, but it's the quality of your close relationships that matters. Living in conflict or within a toxic relationship is more damaging than being alone.

As a society and as individuals, we must urgently prioritise investing in building and maintaining good healthy relationships and tackling the barriers to forming them. Failing to do so is the equivalent to turning a blind eye to the impact of smoking and obesity on our health and wellbeing.

The Mental Health Foundation defines relationships as 'the way in which two or more people are connected, or the state of being connected'. Relationships include the intimate relationships we have with our respective partner, those we form with our parents, siblings and grandparents and those we form socially with our friends, work colleagues, teachers, health care professionals and the community and society at large. Extensive evidence shows that having superior quality relationships can help us live healthier longer lasting lives with fewer mental health problems. Having close, positive relationships can give us a sense of belonging. Loneliness and isolation remain the key predictors for poor psychological and physical health.

Having a lack of excellent quality relationships and long-term feelings of loneliness have been shown by a range of studies to be associated with higher rates of mortality, poor physical health outcomes and lower satisfaction.

In contrast, they were depressed and some suicidal and had similar if not the same kinds of problems as people who were in poor relationships. I asked myself why these millionaires were so depressed, and it was simple, none of them were in lasting relationships sharing their experiences and memories but on their own and feeling lonely.

As a relationship therapist, I found that people are happier when they believe (chapter 9 Mental Law of Belief) their romantic intimate relationships are loving and fulfilling. It is a well-known statistic that people live longer in happy relationships, especially married relationships. Marriage should be about pooling financial resources together, sharing, caring and encouraging each other are healthy, being healthy people live longer as again couples that are feeling contented and happier will automatically have feel good endorphins that enable them to starve off illness and stress than someone dealing with all life's problems on their own.

It does not matter if you have money, if you have no one to share it with. Research shows that if you live your life with someone else you are likely to live longer.

This is due to single people taking more risks. Single people are more likely to burn the candle at both ends, have less sleep and do riskier activities. In contrast, people in long term relationships, marriage or a firm partnership look after each other better, have healthier lifestyles including food and exercise, cooking for each other.

Extrovert single people are more at risk than any other control group and more likely to take extreme risks such as drinking, taking drugs and driving fast. When we come into the world, humans quickly learn to adapt, to compromise and share in all walks of life from work, relationships families and friends. In short, if you don't, you alienate yourself and simply don't have many friends. Therefore, we have learnt sharing is vital to success and to be popular.

In my work as a relationship therapist, I also use a theory called social exchange theory. Social exchange theory focusses on the outcomes of a relationship where a partner focuses on outcomes (rewards) and negative outcomes (costs) of their relationship. Rewards include social rewards and material rewards. Costs include opportunity costs. A similar theory, equity theory, focuses on that not all relationships are equal and need rebalancing to avoid resentment jealousy and envy. Using these theories coupled with couples counselling enables individuals to share and learn empathy of what it is like to be in the shoes of the other person and find compromise. Trust is the foundation of the relationship, but this is built on honesty and sharing and developing, encouraging and supporting each other through sickness and health, richer and poorer.

This is no more evident than couples carrying out prenups before getting married, equality and social exchange theory goes out of the window and the person on the receiving end feels resentful and lack of trust. Studies have shown recently that 64% of couples that do a prenup end in divorce compared to 47% that chose to share all. Studies also show that couples without a prenup live happier and healthier life styles than the stress of that piece of paper sitting in a draw like a ticking time bomb. I believe the key to a successful relationship is to compromise, as well as sharing encouraging, supporting and listening to each other regardless of the partner's situation will lead to longevity.

Chapter 16
Happiness Is Found in Attracting Like-minded People

For me, happiness is achieved through meeting the right kind of people that enrich your lives. I call this likeminded people. Like-minded people who share the same beliefs, values and expectations with others. Going back to the mental laws such as belief, expectation and attraction we can live our life like we lived before by being wiser through sharing it with people that share our values. This will attract us to like-minded people who want to lead fulfilling, positive lives and be successful and the best they can be. With the law of attraction like is attracted to like, therefore likeminded people will be attracted to like-minded people. However, this can both be a cause and effect that is either positive or negative. Just as positive like-minded people are attracted to like-minded positive values and beliefs and expectations, equally like-minded people who share a commonality of negativity can also be attracted to other negative thinking people. The title, *Live Your Life like You Have Lived It Before* is to be aware not to make mistakes in meeting negative people who share and project negative values. For example, not using these ideas you can easily fall into the trap that many people make and meet like-minded negative people who cause unhappiness, failure, bad vibes, stress and lead unhealthy life styles.

It was important for me that this book was not about money but clearly your life style, class and equality of opportunity will play massive roles in financial opportunity. However, this material will give you the choice and chance to avoid making which may be deemed poor decisions that have bad outcomes which may cause financial problems. It is vital you have the knowledge to know how dangerous it can be meeting someone who brings you down and makes you unhappy.

My dad once said to me, "Once you are with someone with problems they become your problems." How true that simple statement is. In my therapy room this is sadly why there is a direct correlation and connection between people with depression or being victims of domestic violence and or abuse that can unfortunately be attracted to people who have experienced these kind of life experiences. It does not always by happen by accident and bad luck, it's the law of attraction working from being in an unfortunate negative cycle that needs to be broken. However, studies as well as real life experiences reported have shown that it is extremely difficult to leave an abusive relationship due to learnt helplessness, false projection of believing that they somehow deserve it, causing very low esteem created by exposure to this oppressive living. It is vital to break free and be brave and learn you deserve better and to be happy, which starts with therapy to improve self-esteem and belief of self-worth. However, as well as this, worse still, the negative impact of the law of attraction attracting like-minded people is also why people who have sadly been abused can fall for another abuser or be in controlling oppressive relationships through learnt behaviour of low self-esteem caused by their negative abuser ruining their life. There are cases and considerable research to show that why and how they can become an abuser themselves.

There are also many arguments regarding nature and nurture that our experiences are down to upbringing, class, who our families are, if we start rich or poor background with better opportunities than people in lower class backgrounds. They call this equality of opportunity in sociology. Linked to nature is nurture of course and in short, how hard you work with whatever opportunities you have from your upbringing.

However, all this for me it is much simpler, and I believe by changing your thinking, attitude, beliefs, expectations and set clear goals, you can frankly achieve anything you want to and fulfil all your hopes and dreams. However, it is attachments from John Bowlby, attachment theory of either a secure or insecure attachment that plays a vital part and is the key to who we may end up with as a partner. Our style of attachment affects everything from our partner selection to how well our relationship progresses to sadly how they end. That is why recognising our attachment pattern can help us understand our strengths and vulnerabilities in a relationship.

An attachment pattern is established in early childhood attachments continue to function as a working model for relationships in adulthood. What Bowlby describes as a secure attachment will result in a confident person who is easy to react with and able to meet their partner's needs. In contrast, an anxious avoidant attachment and person picks a partner who fits the maladaptive pattern and most likely will choose a person who isn't the ideal choice to making them happy and contented and likely to be unhappy and lead unfulfilled lives. We seem to duplicate these models even if our patterns of attachment will result in us being attached to a like-minded negative person who may hurt us and make us unhappy. For example, a person with a preoccupied attachment feels that to get close to someone and have their needs meet yours need a partner all the time to reassure you. This kind of relationship will result in a person supporting this perception of reality by choosing someone who is isolated and hard to connect with.

A person with a dismissive avoidant attachment has the tendency to distance themselves and in short you won't get your needs met, as you are seen that you don't have any. He or she will choose someone who is possessive or overtly demanding of attention. The key therefore is awareness to recognise our patterns and change our thinking and beliefs to meet more positive people and have better outcomes and success in life.

The good news with negative thinking is it can be changed, and I believe not always by therapy but by working positively if you do something about changing your thinking and changing your life and challenging your negative thinking or automatic negative thoughts you can meet positive and happy fulfilled people and lead successful and healthy lives. To meet the right kind of people, you should have positive values, beliefs and expectations in yourself and your ability, so that is why the material in this book is so important to avoid the mistakes many of us make and are attracted to negative people which causes negative experiences and memories stress, depression, anxiety and early death.

To get out of this cycle is mainly to do with low self-esteem and building this up by believing in yourself and your abilities and by following other chapters, smiling displays confidence and transforming your negative automatic thoughts to *CAN DO* attitude and you are then more likely to attract a future partner who sees the new you with a halo of positive belief in yourself and will come over and talk to you rather than someone who has developed negative attitude and likely formed insecure attachments and low self-esteem. The important part is, I believe, everyone can change despite all the negative attitudes and beliefs people can't change. "You can't get a horse to drink water." Through observing people through life, my own lived experiences and through my therapy, I believe you can. I believe anything is possible. We can all change if we want to or make a **choice** to change our thinking. Through my sessions and gratitude therapy, I enable people who have developed negative thoughts through some awful life experiences to rebuild their self-esteem, improve informed choices equality and confidence to meet more positive likeminded people by following just some of these steps in this book.

Both men and women of cosmopolitan diverse cultures and backgrounds and people from the LGBT community have changed there thinking through following a handful of exercises, and again the material in this book. As an experienced mental health professional and relationship therapist, I believe this book will help you meet likeminded people and live your life like you have already lived it before all over the world who want to lead fulfilling happy lives. Remember we are all unique individuals which through this uniqueness radiate creativity. To me, this uniqueness makes us capable of doing amazing and wonderful things in our life.

Chapter 17
Bringing It All Together

The key to the material in this book is bringing it all together. When I used to study with the University it did not make sense until all the modules were brought together, and you could clearly see how everything I learnt was connected.

Now I have reached the milestone of the big 50, I don't want you to make the same mistakes as me and others. I want you to have the tools now to enable you and others to lead fulfilling lives, rich with endless possibilities. I want you to be successful in relationships, career, money and above all else live your life like you have lived it before. I don't want you to make mistakes and learn the hard way with all the stress attached to these experiences in life.

As a therapist for many years, I want to give you as unique individuals the mental tools and strategies and not waste the remarkable gift of life for you to fulfil your potential immediately. As I mentioned, every chapter is linked. As humans we are linked and connected. The heaven, the earth, water, the trees the animals, evolution and the food chain. Mankind is also trying to get by and learn and develop and improve and seek and search for the Holy Grail how to be successful and happy I explained in chapter 3, everyone is searching for something. Think how powerful if you have lived your life like you lived it before and already have the tool given as a gift in this book. Remember to understand that people desire what they can't have and that it is okay to not always get what you desire but maybe as the song goes what you need, you may feel an argument brewing and then remember *no action is action itself,* chapter 5, and as a result are still in the relationship perhaps now married. Knowing *it's okay to make mistakes*, chapter 2, like many genius's and famous people who changed their thinking to be successful. In short failure increases your chances of success.

Although we *desire what we can't have*, chapter 4, is vital to learn that we can't always have everything we desire in life or we will be set up to fail and this will cause unhappiness but It's also important to understand that people desire you more if they can't have you. You are, all of you, unique human beings capable of extraordinary thing and therefore use that uniqueness to *stand out from the crowd*, chapter 6, and do it differently and be comfortable with who you are, your identity personality and own skin. Just as we are unique we have a history and through evolution of being saviours to be *resilient*, chapter 8. We have natural ability to survive and keep us safe and secure as hunter gatherers. Remember *goals are not goals if you don't write them down*, chapter 10. You be amazed how quickly you will achieve by having a plan and make your hopes and dreams a reality.

Remember to give, not just at Christmas but through volunteering, just see how powerful it is to *give and karma will give it back*, Chapter 14, will look after you the rest of your life. I deliberately did not do a chapter on money and how to make money, as there are plenty of books about this some better than others, but I feel the *quality of your relationships defines us*, chapter 15, and most importantly success.

Finally, remember to *count your blessing and go back to nature*, chapter 12. You can do this by being mindful everywhere you are, a walk in the forest or by the seaside, at work you can always see beauty in nature and the world if you change your thinking and look for it. These positive attitudes will enable you to have *a healthy self-concept*, chapter 7, by being confident and at the same time make you happy and contented and believe in yourself and your ability. Remember *life is not a dress rehearsal so don't waste it*, chapter 13.

Remember to *laugh and success will smile on you*, chapter 11, and why there are therapies on this such as laughing therapy. It is amazing even under the most adverse conditions and life experiences how this can improve your mental health and wellbeing and studies have shown that laughter can prevent stress, depression and anxiety and heart disease and prolong life.

Think how powerful you now are and will become armed with all this connected knowledge before you have even started and what an advantage you hold over others without this knowledge and wisdom to be successful and lead fulfilling lives.

I believe you will do things in this book and when you realise that they make a difference in your lives even though they are connected, you will be not even thinking about the connections and just doing it and by doing it lead happy and successful lives by being new positive thinkers with the belief in yourself and expectation of only good things will happen to you on your journey of life. So, I wish you well on your life journey and hope that you use some of the material in this book to live your Life like you have lived it before and I look forward to hearing good positive stories that have happened to you in your life. Life is so short and being short you have not got the time to waste and make mistakes and bad decisions, meet negative people which cause chaos in your life and before you know it you are old and grey, and your life is all over. I want this book to give you the tools to learn quickly and be the best you can become. I want you to *attract likeminded people*, chapter 16, and in doing so meet good people and have exciting opportunities, have doors open to you and success shine on you. So, Go forward and prosper and change your thinking and *transform your life*, chapter 1.

Believe in yourself and expect good things to happen to you and you will live your life like you have lived it before just like me. I started to change my thinking and lived my life like I lived it before and where I wrote this book on my boat from watching and listening to nature in beautiful surroundings and through mindful experience learnt to live again and be resilient and change my thinking.

Most importantly, when I started to put my ideas into writing this book wonderful things started to happen to me, the most important of all which I believe you can truly measure *success is by the quality of your relationships*, chapter 15. There is no better relationship than a romantic, one, my new *thinking attracted me to a like-minded person*, chapter 16, who shared my values and who, on 2nd June 2017, I got married to and consider the love of my life. So, changing my thinking, I met the loveliest, like-minded person that shares all my hopes, dreams and values, my beautiful wife. So, if it works for me then it will work for you and you will live your life like you have lived it before. I hope the mental laws of the universe in chapter 9 *beliefs, expectations and attraction* brings you new confidence and self-esteem that you like yourself as let's face it everyone wants to feel liked and that this new *change in thinking will simply transforms your life*, chapter 1.

Go and write down today some new goals, chapter 10, and be successful through your new positive thinking that you can achieve anything and attract wonderful energy and an abundance of happiness, fulfilment, success and meet likeminded people who share your new wisdom of life. Most importantly, please like yourself and vitally love yourself. *Yes, love yourself.*

Self-love is the most important thing you can do. Self-love for yourself because you need to love yourself to love others. It is important to feel worthy and value yourself as well as others and it creates belief in yourself and confidence. So, let's be clear, as I sign off, I value all of you and care about what happens to you in your life. I wanted to give you the secrets of success to lead a fulfilling happy contented life and find peace of mind that you are on the right positive path on your journey of life.

As Mary Poppings would say, "Be Super Not Superficial." In a world of Microblading, Botox and pressure to be a size zero, I believe this will not make you happy. As well as being good, it has already shown that social media can cause harm. A recent comprehensive study by the Royal Society for public health speaking to young people between 14 to 25 years of age in April 2018 showed evidence the harm social media does to young people. Today, young people especially feel the need to have more fake friends, most that they have never talked to before and / or send selfies of themselves posing on holiday. This need to be liked even by people you will never meet has caused psychological and mental health problems, identity issues, eating disorders, bullying and even suicide. Therefore, it is vital to be yourself and not be pressurised into the world of fake and false and superficial such as in the beauty industry, injecting yourself with Botox or needing to have false hair extensions, false eye lashes or sadly even surgery to stay or make yourself feel younger and happier. I believe if others can't accept you for who you are then they are simply not right for you. Therefore, be yourself and true to who you are and accept yourself and be comfortable in your skin. If you can do this you will have peace of mind, feel contented, fulfilled and happy, and you will like and love yourself as a unique, beautiful individual you truly are. Then others will like and love you for who you are as well.

Life is not a sprint but a marathon but wouldn't it better to set off from the starting gate with a plan and wisdom to be successful and live your life like you have lived it before rather than randomly winging it and making mistakes that have consequences for your future happiness.

With that in mind, I believe in you and value all of you and care for what happens to all people who read this book and put it into positive action to improve the quality of their lives. Therefore, I am available to be contacted below, and I will try to respond to all your comments and look forward to hearing your success stories after reading my book.

Bibliography

Books used

Jeremy Holmes, *John Bowlby and Attachment Theory,* Routledge, 1993

Brian Tracy, *Maximum Achievement,* Simon and Schuster, 1993

Zig Ziglar, *Goals: Setting and Achieving Them on Schedule,* Simon and Schuster, 1998

Websites used

Searching for: Happiness Quotes (7 quotes) – Goodreads

Giving to Receive: 10 Practices Using the Law of Karma | The Chopra…
https://chopra.com/articles/giving-to-receive-10-practices-using-the-law-of-karma

Why We Want the Person We Can't Have, According to Science
https://www.brainyquote.com/quotes/harvey_mackay_528743

Relationships | Psychology Today
https://www.psychologytoday.com/us/basics/relationships

Inaction Quotes (96 quotes) – Goodreads
https://www.goodreads.com/quotes/tag/inaction

What is Gratitude and What Is its Role in Positive Psychology?
https://positivepsychologyprogram.com/gratitude-appreciation

WHO | Fact sheets on mental health – World Health Organization
www.who.int/campaigns/world-health-day/2017/fact-sheets/en

Thank you for reading my self-help book, and I hope it has made a difference to the quality of your life. Good luck everyone and go for it! Live your life like you have always wanted. Whatever has happened in your life from now on is a fresh start of positive change of new expectations, beliefs and you will attract an abundance of amazing energy to achieve everything you want and need by using this book as a reference. So, go for it, let it happen and believe in your abilities and if you do you will…

"Live your life as you have lived it before." Bateup M 2016
Malcolm Bateup BSC Hon psych Ad Dip CP MNCS

Website: www.mbc-relationships.co.uk
Or www.mbcounselling-sussex.com
Blog: mbc-relationships.co.uk/blog
Gmail: MBCounselling2@gmail.com
Email: malcolmbateup77@yahoo.co.uk

"Every Life Matters"

Special dedication in the memory of
Mark Mathura

If life is difficult and you are not in a good place and maybe feeling suicidal, then please speak to someone as talking saves lives and simply because every life matters.

Where to get help

The Samaritans
Samaritans.org
Helpline 116 123
24 hours a day, 7 hours a week

The Royal college of Psychiatrists
Rcpsych.ac.uk

Self-Management UK
Selfmanagementuk.org

Time to Talk
www.sussexcommunity.nhs/timetotalk

Time to Change
Time-to-change.org.uk

Sussex Oakleaf
www.sussexoakleaf.org.uk

Recovery support for people with mental health problems.
www.nhs.uk
Mental Health Lines NHS

Anxiety UK
Charity providing support if you are diagnosed with an
anxiety condition
Telephone 03444 775 744

Depression Alliance
Charity for sufferers of depression. Has network of self-help
groups.
Website www.depressionalliance.org.uk

PAPYRUS
Young suicide prevention society
Telephone HOPE line 0800 068 4141
Website www.papyrus-uk.org

Rethink
Support and advice for people living with mental illness
Telephone 0300 5000 927
Website www.rethink.org

SANE
Emotional support information and guidance for people
affected by mental illness their families and carers.
SANEline 0300 304 7000
www.sane.org.uk

Mental Health Foundation
Mental Health Foundation provides a guide to Mental Health
problems, topical issues and treatment options via their
website.
Visit the Mental Health Foundation website

Mind
Mind.org.uk
Helpline 0300 123 3393
Mind provides advice and support on a range of topics
including types of mental health problem, legislation and
details of local help and support in England and Wales.
Phone: 0300 123 3393 (weekdays 9am–6pm)
Visit the Mind website

Young Minds
Young Minds offers information, support and advice for
children and young people.
Help for concerned parents of those under 25 is offered by
phone.
Phone: 0808 802 5544 (Mon–Fri 9.30am-4pm)
Visit the Young Minds website

Anxiety UK
Supporting people affected by Anxiety
Anxietyuk.org.uk
Helpline 08444 775 774
Text 07537 416 905

Beat
Supporting people affected by Eating disorders
Beateatingdisorders.org.uk
Helpline 0808 801 0677

PANDAS Foundation
Supporting people affected by pre and post-natal depression
Pandasfoundation.org.uk
Mental Health Line
0300 500 0101
Helpline 0843 28 98 401

Inspire

Inspire (Northern Ireland Association for Mental Health) provides local services to support the mental health and wellbeing of people across Northern Ireland.
Phone: 028 9032 8474
Visit the Inspire website

SAMH
SAMH (Scottish Association for Mental Health) can provide general mental health information and signpost you to your local services.
Phone: 0141 530 1000 (Mon-Fri 9–5)
Visit the SAMH website

Community Advice & Listening Line
Community Advice & Listening Line offers emotional support and information on mental health and related matters to people in Wales.
Phone: 0800 132 737 (24/7) or text "help" to 81066

'Remember whoever you are, we are all God's children, so God bless you all, and go and live your life like you have lived it before.'